PRICE
AND
VALUATION

A way to determine the actual price of a company
and the associated common stock

Nicholas Jewczyn, Ph.D.

authorHOUSE®

AuthorHouse™ LLC
1663 Liberty Drive
Bloomington, IN 47403
www.authorhouse.com
Phone: 1-800-839-8640

Published by AuthorHouse 12/16/2013

ISBN: 978-1-4918-4542-4 (sc)
ISBN: 978-1-4918-4543-1 (e)

Library of Congress Control Number: 2013923181

Walden University

College of Management and Technology

This is to certify that the doctoral dissertation by

Nicholas Jewczyn

has been found to be complete and satisfactory in all respects,
and that any and all revisions required by
the review committee have been made.

Review Committee
Dr. Mohammad Sharifzadeh, Committee Chairperson, Management Faculty
Dr. Robert Aubey, Committee Member, Management Faculty
Dr. William Brent, University Reviewer, Management Faculty

Chief Academic Officer
Eric Riedel, Ph.D.

Walden University
2013

Abstract

Relative Pricing of Publicly Traded U.S. Electric Utility Company Securities

by

Nicholas Stephen Jewczyn

MBA, New York Institute of Technology, 2008

BS, Southern Illinois University at Carbondale, 1984

Dissertation Submitted in Partial Fulfillment

of the Requirements for the Degree of

Doctor of Philosophy

Management

Walden University

August 2013

Abstract

In the financial turmoil of 2008, U.S. firms reported debt-ratios that differed from the debt-ratios calculated from balance sheets. The problem is that investors bought common stock expecting initial investment return and lost money when companies delisted. The purpose of this quantitative study was to determine sample securities pricing with the application of synthetic assets and debt accrued. Addressed in the research questions was whether those securities were (a) underpriced compared with return-on-assets (ROA), (b) overpriced compared with ROA, (c) a debt-ratio higher than 60% and also overpriced, (d) underpriced with a synthetic asset added, or (e) related by relative pricing to variant pricing and market capitalization. The study's base theory was Pan's efficient market hypothesis (EMH) of security price prediction of market prices versus model prices. The data from the financial statements of 16 publicly traded U.S. electric utility companies were analyzed via correlations and multiple regression analyses to determine securities pricing and suitability. The findings from the analyses of the sample's variables of market price, book value, market-to-book, and study constructed variables from those variable data were statistically significant. The alternate hypotheses were accepted for all 5 research questions since the analytical operationalization of the hypothetical constructs led to significant relationships. Results suggest that the use of more pricing determinants in securities evaluation may lead to investors losing less money and earning the expected returns for a more efficient capital market, leading to a stronger economy and macroeconomic stability.

Relative Pricing of Publicly Traded U.S. Electric Utility Companies

by

Nicholas Stephen Jewczyn

MBA, New York Institute of Technology, 2008

BS, Southern Illinois University at Carbondale, 1984

Dissertation Submitted in Partial Fulfillment

of the Requirements for the Degree of

Doctor of Philosophy

Management – Financial Economics (Self-Designed)

Walden University

August 2013

Dedication

My dissertation work is dedicated to the Great Geometer of the Universe and to my fraternal brothers, my family, and my friends who supported me from the beginning.

This capstone achievement would not have been possible without the divine inspiration necessary to proceed because the super-conscious has always provided speedy solutions to difficulties posed; my belief in the Great Geometer and my travel East never faltered. I want to thank my mother Anastasia Shamro Jewczyn for pushing me hard in the academics of my formative years where a great relish for learning was fostered and then was meticulously grown. I would like to thank all of my mentors, peers, colleagues, and friends for their unshakable belief in my ultimate and unfettered success. There were many who have been included in that just mentioned group, but I would particularly like to thank my colleague and long-time friend Dr. Karl Senawi for his incredible zeal in learning, Mr. J. Mark Crews for his practitioner-based advice from the Field of Finance, the Rosemark Council #131 Illustrious Master Br. Fred Howard for my perspective relating to humanity and the Great Geometer, and Editor-in-Chief Dr. Marty Ludlum who got me started publishing in a variety of peer-reviewed, Cabell's-rated journals. I also want to thank my wife Cynthia Louise Jewczyn of many years, with whom I share in the delight of two children and two grandchildren, for being a true partner making my life worth living and for not giving up on me during this arduous and lengthy process. Without the work that was started by my mother, prayerfully advanced by my wife, and cemented by my dissertation committee, this work result would not have been possible.

Acknowledgments

I would like to thank the faculty and support staff below for their extraordinary help in positioning me to achieve these most excellent academic results:

Dr. Mohammad Sharifzadeh, Committee Chair and Methodology Expert, who as my mentor was expeditious in moving my Knowledge Area Module (KAM) demonstrations, which were upper-tier Bloom's Taxonomy individual 125-page written, critical analyses of a subject area's base theory, current literature, and a resultant theoretical application construct, forward to completion and who as my chair was instrumental in helping me to develop my dissertation with noteworthy revisions. Dr. Mohammad, you are certainly "one-in-a-million."

Dr. Robert Aubey, Committee Member and Content Expert, I appreciate your expeditious revisions and dedication during the dissertation review process.

Dr. William Brent, University Research Reviewer, your feedback and help during my dissertation process was greatly appreciated.

Sarah Matthey from the Research and Writing Center for form and style edits.

Thank you!

"Completing this work with zeal was the only option…"

About the Author

Dr. Jewczyn grew up as a farm kid in upstate New York and, after a stint as a radio D.J., served six years in the U.S. Navy as a Navy Corpsman and Pharmacist's Mate (running the busiest military pharmacy on earth). He completed his baccalaureate degree in 16 months, using the Montgomery G.I. Bill. He earned the degree while working full-time on active duty. After a stint in the Navy's Sixth Fleet (Admiral's Staff) on an aircraft carrier as the Pharmacy representative to a Rapid Deployment Surgical Team (the first "normalization cruise" after the Beirut bombing in 1983 - a diplomatic mission), Dr. Jewczyn completed his Navy tour and became an insurance agent and a securities registered representative for the wealthiest company on earth. For over 20 years, Dr. Jewczyn worked in or around the finance industry as a business owner, factor, business consultant, financial advisor, and federal judge for the securities industry, to make sure that investors received good value and that institutions grew with good business practices. As a student, Dr. Jewczyn has enrolled for and taken over 400 semester hours of college classes and as an instructor he has served as a department chair, course architect, and a curriculum developer - he has taught over two-dozen college classes in accounting, business, economics, and finance. His Master of Business Administration/ Finance (with Distinction) and Doctor of Philosophy with a specialization in Financial Economics (Honors Graduate) degrees and his considerable practitioner experience in the real world have prepared him to write extraordinary texts and international academic journal research articles in economics and finance. He lives with his family in San Diego, CA and serves as a Professor of Finance at a major university (70,000+ students). His hobbies include kayaking in Mission Bay, lap swimming, SCUBA, real-time computer strategy war-gaming, and jogging on the beaches at Coronado Island.

Table of Contents

xv

List of Tables

List of Figures

Chapter 1: Introduction to the Study

Introduction

The intent of the study was to determine a means of relative (Damodaran, 2006, p. 15) firm valuation and securities repricing for all investors. The repricing was accomplished by examining the relationship between any combination of firm valuation variables using market value, book value, and return-on-assets (ROA) (Chou, Chou, & Ko, 2009, p. 193). The examination enabled the finding of high market-to-book value (Shim, Siegel, & Lansner, 1994, p. 150), publicly-traded U.S. electric utility companies in a manner different from traditional techniques for such electric company valuation (Wang, 2008, p. 546). The finding of such high market-to-book value companies through this study might have led to the creation of a model to be used to determine the amount of synthetic assets necessary (Gubler, 2011, p. 68), with the use of derivatives (Gubler, 2011, p. 97), to reorient those companies' debt-ratios because the amount of company debt directly bears upon short-term performance and returns (Ozel, 2010, p. i). This short-term business revaluation intercession might be the impetus necessary to eliminate investor satiation and promote an investors' resurgence of capital direct investment in those companies (Rondinelli & Burpitt, 2000, p. 181). Once investor capital movement has reoriented the company to a low market-to-book value company, the need for the synthetic assets would have been eliminated and the derivative positions could be closed. The theory proposed above has larger societal applications for the evaluation of all securities (inferential) in the marketplace with regard to firm revaluation, the repricing of the associated securities, and the prospective inclusion of those securities in a private investor or institutional investment portfolio.

The study was based research that included the variables of market value-to-book value (MVBV) and return-on-assets (ROA). Relationships have been established between MVBV and the return-on-equity (ROE) variables (Prado-Lorenzo, Rodriguez-Dominguez, Gallego-Alvarez, & Garcia-Sanchez, 2009, p. 1143), but no investigator has combined MVBV and ROA in publicly-traded U.S. electric utility companies. Associated work has been done concerning diversification and firm performance with the variables of "Return on Assets (ROA), Return on Equity (ROE), [and] Market Rate of Return (MKRT) (Afza, Slahudin, & Nazir, 2008, p. 7), future book-to-market and ROE (Clubb & Naffi, 2007, p. 1), and the profit measures of ROA and ROE along with market measures such as market return (Gentry & Shen, 2010, p. 514). Related work has been done with computer models based upon ROA, ROE, and MVBV (Prado-Lorenzo et al. 2009, p. 1133), *ex-ante* and *ex-post* capital valuation from the traditional capital asset pricing model (CAPM), and Fama-French model work (Muiño & Trombetta, 2009, p. 88). There was work regarding scholar disagreements regarding traditional models, ROE and ROA, and firm valuation (Rachdi & Ameur, 2011, p. 88) that prompted the use of multiple methodological tools for analysis in this study.

In this study, I discussed the derivative-induced, synthetic assets to improve the nontraditional, relative firm revaluation and the associated securities repricing of publicly traded U.S. electric utility companies. I wished to determine if there was a relationship between MVBV and ROA for publicly traded U.S. electric utility companies

such that a treatment with a study-based Excel computer model process could be used to

change a company's debt-ratio to promote investor initial investment. The promotion of

investor initial investment is important because firms must compete for funds to grow,

because investors have alternative choices for investment funds (Mondher, 2011, p. 194),

and the amount of leverage in a firm, more commonly known as the debt-ratio, does

affect investor investment (Mondher, 2011, p. 194). In this chapter, I present the problem

statement, problem background, nature of the study, purpose statement, research

questions and hypotheses, study basis, terms, assumptions, scope and delimitations,

limitations, significance of the study, and a summary.

Statement of the Problem

The general problem was that investors invested an initial investment in publicly-

traded common stock and expected the eventual recovery of the initial investment, which

was not the case when the companies underlying the purchased securities were delisted

from securities exchanges (Armstrong, Davila, Foster, & Hand, 2011, p. 52). The specific

problem was that investors lost their initial investment and the associated investment

securities profits, even though investors expected an initial investment to be repaid along

with an investment profit for an expected return (Haymore, 2011, p. 1312). The problem

analysis involved publicly-traded U.S. electric utility companies' data because such

utilities were found to be integral to the U.S. economy (McGowan, 2011, para. 3).

Prudent investors would not overpay for an initial investment in a company's security, but hypothetical models in studies were shown to overvalue prospective

investor payments for publicly-traded securities that were model calculated to be

overpriced (Morrison & Brown, 2009, p. 307). The Stage 1 security relative pricing

revealed priced publicly-traded U.S. electric utility companies that provided electricity

resources. The company securities were computer model study process repriced in Stage

2 to reflect the actual debt accrued but not completely reported by the underlying

company (Arends, 2010, para 1, 6) to give investors better value for their initial

investment.

Relationships have already been established between MVBV and the ROE

variables (Prado-Lorenzo et al., 2009, p. 1143), but no investigator has combined MVBV

and ROA in publicly-traded U.S. electric utility companies. In this study, I wished to

determine if a relationship between MVBV and ROA for publicly-traded U.S. electric

utility companies for treatment with a study-based Excel computer model process to

change a company's debt-ratio promoted investor initial investment.

Background of the Problem

Traditional pricing techniques (Grauer, 2008, p. 150) are not always acceptable

for the pricing of securities (Johnstone, 2007, p. 159). For some equity pricing instances,

the "price to book value [MVBV] is the best standalone price multiple" (Sehgal &

Pandey, 2010, p. 68). Relationships have been established between market value, book

value and ROE variables (Prado-Lorenzo et al. 2009, p. 1143), but no researcher has used

market value, book value, and ROA in publicly-traded U.S. electric utility companies.

The use of ROA to determine corporate pricing was found to still be valid (Alkhalialeh, 2008, p. 246). These observations supported the use of book value, market value, and ROA variables. The usage in the study of company security risk *beta*, market capitalization, and assets impairment was consistent with the usage of control variables in statistical analysis (Berkman & Reise, 2012, p. 207).

The relative pricing of publicly-traded U.S. electric utility companies allowed a determination of the presence of overpriced companies differently from traditional pricing techniques (Wang, 2008, p. 546). The finding of overpriced sample companies guided the use of a study-based Excel computer model process for the synthetic assets necessary (Gubler, 2011, p. 68), using derivatives (Gubler, 2011, p. 97), to reduce those companies' debt-ratios. A reduced debt-ratio was found to be important because the debt-ratio bears upon company performance and security returns (Ozel, 2010, p. i).

The sample companies' study repricing could raise the level of investor satiation and promote an investors' resurgence of capital direct investment into publicly-traded U.S. electric utility companies (Hackmann, Yi, & Valeva, 2010, p. 15). The study securities repricing has larger societal applications for the repricing of all marketplace securities and the potential inclusion of those securities in investment portfolios.

Nature of the Study

Companies in the United States were found to be holding the largest amount of corporate debt in recorded history, amounting to $7.2 trillion when compared with the amount of their corporate equity held of $1.8 trillion in cash, so that these companies' average debt-ratio was 80% (Arends, 2010, para 1, 6). The optimal debt-ratio for many publicly-traded companies should be between the debt-ratio limits of 30% and 60% (Eiteman, Stonehill, & Moffett, 2007, p. 434). Publicly traded U.S. electric utility companies were chosen as the population for this study because this particular type of electric company was found to generate the electricity consumed by approximately three out of four people in the United States (McNerney, 2007, para 15). Electricity in the United States was found to be integral to the maintenance of the nation's infrastructure for the public sector, and the loss of the generating capacity provided by publicly-traded U.S. electric utility companies would be catastrophic to the nation (McGowan, 2011, para 3).

Eiteman et al. (2007) noted that, for the optimal 30% to 60% debt ratio range noted above, the cost of equity ranged from about 15% to 19%, but that the cost of low-cost, tax-deductible debt, for the same debt ratio range, was only 6% to 8% (p. 435). This circumstance could lead a businessperson to accrue corporate debt, versus the use of equity, in order to expand a company (Arends, 2010, para 1, 6).

Purpose of the Study

The purpose of this quantitative study was to determine the company pricing and securities investment suitability of a randomly selected sample of 16 publicly-traded U.S. electric utility companies. The study design included correlations and multiple regression analyses to support the three-factor, Fama-French, multiple regression model (Muiño & Trombetta, 2009, p. 88). No survey instrument was used because the data were randomly collected from the geographic population of the 160 publicly-traded U.S. electric

utility companies in the Electronic Data Gathering, Analysis, and Retrieval (EDGAR)

database. Data reliability was supported by federal law compliance in the reporting of

each firm's annual 10-K. A validity threat could have been the value-weighting of

security portfolios in the Fama-French regression equation (You & Zhang, 2009, p. 574),

but portfolio security holding compensated for that concern and cross-sectional data

analysis negated unnatural portfolio variance returns (You & Zhang, 2009, p. 575).

Research Questions and Hypotheses

The earning of an economic profit meant that the publicly-traded U.S. electric

utility company made profits above and beyond the company's basic cost of capital,

known as economic value added (EVA), which eventually resulted in higher future

company profitability (Abdel-Jalil & Thuniebat, 2009, p. 26). The stated earnings would

have to have been (per year) more than the static required return on invested capital.

There were five sets of hypotheses. The first set dealt with an underpriced

situation compared with ROA. The second set dealt with overpriced results compared

with ROA. The third set dealt with whether a publicly-traded U.S. electric utility

company, with a debt-ratio higher than the ideal range upper limit of 60% (Eiteman et al.,

2007, p. 434), was the same as an overpriced, publicly-traded U.S. electric utility

company. The fourth set dealt with whether or not a derivative induced, synthetically

created asset would move a publicly-traded U.S. electric utility company from an

overpriced to an underpriced status. The fifth set dealt with whether there was a relationship between a publicly-traded U.S. electric utility company's

nontraditional, relative pricing, a study derived computer model's variant pricing of the

company, and the company's market capitalization (please see Appendix A).

1.   What was the relationship between low market-to-book value (threshold -

the market-to-book ratio is a ratio less than 1:1) publicly-traded U.S.

electric utility companies and their 3-year annualized average return on

assets?

$H_0 1$: There is no relationship between low market-to-book value (threshold - the

market-to-book ratio is a ratio less than 1:1) publicly-traded U.S. electric utility

companies and their 3-year annualized average return on assets.

$H_1 1$: There is a relationship between low market-to-book value (threshold - the

market-to-book ratio is a ratio less than 1:1) publicly-traded U.S. electric utility

companies and their 3-year annualized average return on assets.

The research design for the first set of hypotheses was to demonstrate, with a two-

tailed, t-test correlation and multivariate and bivariate regression studies, that there was a

relationship between the independent variables of market value and book value to the

dependent variable of ROA.

2.   To what extent was there a relationship between high market-to-book

value (threshold - the market-to-book ratio is a ratio of 1:1 or more)

publicly-traded U.S. electric utility companies and their 3-year annualized

average return on assets?

$H_0 2$: There is no relationship between high market-to-book value (threshold - the market-to-book ratio is a ratio of 1:1 or more) publicly-traded U.S. electric utility companies and their 3-year annualized average return on assets.

$H_1 2$: There is a relationship between high market-to-book value (threshold - the market-to-book ratio is a ratio of 1:1 or more) publicly-traded U.S. electric utility companies and their 3-year annualized average return on assets.

The assembled moderating variable of MVBV and the annual ROA variable, for the 3 years of 2010, 2011, and 2012 for each of the sample's relevant 16 publicly-traded U.S. electric utility companies, was intended to be analyzed with the use of the Pearson's r correlation analysis to operationalize the constructs of the first and the second sets of hypotheses.

3. To what extent was there a relationship between a publicly-traded U.S. electric utility company, which was leveraged above a 60% debt-ratio, and a high market-to-book value (threshold - the market-to-book ratio is a ratio of 1:1 or more) publicly-traded U.S. electric utility company?

$H_0 3$: There is no relationship between a publicly-traded U.S. electric utility company leveraged above 60% and a high market-to-book value publicly-traded U.S. electric utility company.

$H_1 3$: There is a relationship between a publicly-traded U.S. electric utility company leveraged above 60% and a high market-to-book value publicly-traded U.S. electric utility company.

To operationalize the constructs of the third set of hypotheses, with regard to the 16 company sample, the list of companies leveraged above 60% was compared to the list of high market-to-book value companies. Data plugs were used to normalize the data (please see the data handling section of this paper). The means of comparison for the 3 years of 2010, 2011, and 2012, for the relevant sample's 16 publicly-traded U.S. electric utility companies, was an intended study with the use of the Pearson's r correlation analysis to operationalize the constructs of the third set of hypotheses.

4. To what extent was the use of derivatives necessary to move a publicly-traded U.S. electric utility company from a high market-to-book value to a low market-to-book value status?

H_04: There is no relationship between the use of a derivative induced, synthetic asset treatment to move a publicly-traded U.S. electric utility company from a high market-to-book value to a low market-to-book value.

H_14: There is a relationship between the use of a derivative induced, synthetic asset treatment to move a publicly-traded U.S. electric utility company from a high market-to-book value to a low market-to-book value.

The operationalization of the constructs regarding the fourth set of hypotheses was accomplished differently from the operationalization of the previous three sets of hypotheses constructs. The reason for the different approach with the fourth set of hypotheses was that a synthetic asset was created to change the debt-ratio of the firms leveraged above 60% in the 16 company sample of publicly-traded U.S. electric utility companies. A version of the three-factor, Fama-French, multiple regression model was used to operationalize the fourth set of hypotheses constructs (Fama & French, 2004, p. 38). Control variables used in operationalizing the previous three sets of hypotheses with covariance analyses were not necessary to operationalize the fourth set of hypotheses constructs because the use of the Fama-French regression equation took into account the necessary market and firm specific factors by default (Fama & French, 2004, p. 38).

5. To what extent was there a relationship between a publicly-traded U.S. electric utility company's nontraditional, relative pricing, a study derived computer model's variant pricing of the company, and the company's market capitalization (see Appendix A)?

$H_0$5: There is no relationship between a publicly-traded U.S. electric utility company's non-traditional, relative pricing, a study derived computer model's variant pricing of the company, and the company's market capitalization.

$H_1$5: There is a relationship between a publicly-traded U.S. electric utility company's non-traditional, relative pricing, a study derived computer model's variant pricing of the company, and the company's market capitalization.

The fifth set of hypotheses dealt with whether there was a relationship between a publicly-traded U.S. electric utility company's nontraditional, relative pricing, a study derived computer model's variant pricing of the company, and the company's market capitalization (please see Appendix A). The variables to be regressed were the results of the CAPM estimate of a company's security price, for each of the 16 sample companies, the associated variant price that included the accounting for the actual debt accrued by the sample company, and that company's market capitalization figure.

Theoretical Basis of the Study

Researchers in the Field of Finance have claimed that quantitative studies, as opposed to qualitative studies, were generally performed on ratio-scale, financial data because "in the quantitative analysis we can bring the predictions of the theory closer to the observed properties of the data" (Olivero, 2010, p. 403). The high market-to-book value firms were positioned for treatment with a study-based Excel computer model process to rebalance each overleveraged or overpriced company's debt-ratio so that the firm would become an underleveraged or underpriced company. A portion of each company's financials were recast to the reported 50% firms' debt-ratio, in order to attract investors' initial investment.

The research method expanded upon finance theory, regarding the valuation of financial instruments from domestic companies, and this study was a variation of and expansion upon the three-factor, Fama-French, multiple regression technique already in accepted use (Mirza & Afzal, 2011, p. 173). Research has not been performed with a study-based Excel computer model process on publicly-traded U.S. electric utility company securities (Prado-Lorenzo et al., 2009, p. 1133). Furthermore, the research has been performed with MVBV and ROE, but not with MVBV and ROA (Afza, Slahudin,

& Nazir, 2008, p. 7; Clubb & Naffi, 2007, p. 1;Gentry & Shen, 2010, p. 514).

The use of the created synthetic assets' payouts created a positive cash-flow (Chang, 2009, p. 34) so that those derivative-induced assets were created (Chang, 2009, pp. 31-32) to use projected financials. The synthetic assets were subtracted from balance sheet debt to reduce the firm's debt-ratio back to the 50% figure actually reported. The derivatives could also have been used as portfolio insurance to inoculate the firm, thereby protecting it from a drop in asset value, so that the derivatives delivered principal when assets dropped. The capital addition just described was capital infused into a firm's balance sheet to reduce the debt-ratio back to the reported 50 % guideline. This innovation was critical to the second-stage of the study because this innovation allowed the movement and partial recasting of a firm's financial statements so that the sample firm moved from being leveraged above 60 % back to being moderately leveraged at the reported 50 % guideline. The low market-to-book value firm's securities then became a target purchase for prudent, potential investors. These proofs were the second stage of this study and hinged upon the results of the first stage. The first stage *t*-test correlations and regression analyses were conducted regarding the variables of market value, book value, and ROA to benchmark each sample firm's relative valuation.

Definitions of Terms

Book value: An accounting term for the particular amount listed in the accounts or books for an item of owner's equity, a liability, or for an asset (Stickney & Weil, 2003, p. 875).

Economic profit: The minimal level of profits, such that the firm has at zero or positive profits, which allow a firm to remain in business and the term includes income, dollars, and costs of opportunity (Samuelson & Nordhaus, 1995, p. 135).

Impairment: The reduced marketability or value of an asset that occurs when a firm obtains information that long-term assets have lost value in marketability or will provide a reduced return that was not expected (Stickney & Weil, 2003, p. 907).

Investment: Corporate securities, of other companies held by a company for long-term appreciation, which are recorded in a segregated section of the company in question's balance sheet (Stickney & Weil, 2003, p. 911).

Market value: The price agreed upon in the open market between rationally acting buyers and sellers who act in their own best interests (Stickney & Weil, 2003, p. 899).

Optimally leveraged firms: Many publicly traded firms have a debt-ratio of between 30% and 60% to properly use resources and satisfy investors (Eiteman et al., 2007, p. 434).

Overleveraged firms: Firms that have a debt-ratio higher than 60% (Eiteman et al. 2007, p. 434).

Principal: The base amount of funding that is used to tabulate interest (Stickney & Weil, 2003, p. 927).

Return-on-assets (ROA): Also known as the return on total assets, it is the annual net operating income divided by the amount of the annual, averaged total assets (Heintz & Parry, 2008, pp. 954-955).

15

Return-on-investment (ROI): The gross amount of revenue for a period of time before any payments to investors; the rate calculated by dividing this particular figure by the average of total assets (Stickney & Weil, 2003, p. 935).

Synthetic asset: An asset that is created from the grouping of two or more preexisting financial products (Gubler, 2011, pp. 96-97).

Undervalued firm: A firm that may be a good buy for a potential investor because the market value per share is lower than the book value per share (Shim et al., 1994, p. 150).

Valuation: An estimation of worth; in this context used in relation to a corporate entity or investment instrument to which could be applied one of the three valuation techniques known as discounted cash flow (DCF), relative valuation (RV), or contingent claim (CV) (Damodaran, 2006, p. 9).

Assumptions

One of the assumptions of this study was to use a reverse order of magnitude (a reduction of the population by one order of magnitude, or a factor of 10), so that inferential statistics were used for generalization of the results in Chapter Four of the dissertation manuscript (DM) to relate the sample's results to the population sampled (Creswell, 2009, p. 148). In this particular case, a company sample size of 16 publicly-traded U.S. electric utility companies for comparison to a population of 160 publicly-traded U.S. electric utility companies was appropriate. One means of verifying the correlation's accuracy for some hypotheses was the Durbin-Watson test for "first-order error autocorrelation" (Aczel & Sounderpandian, 2009, p. 540), wherein the given statistical alpha's level examined for that α was 0.05. The observed correlation was large enough so that the $p1$ value would be smaller than the alpha 0.05 threshold noted above so that the p-value was be $p1 < 0$ or $p1 > 0$ (two critical points). The autocorrelation, in the case of a resulting positive correlation, reinforced the previously discussed magnitude assumption for the study's generalization of results from the sample to the population.

No survey instrument, preexisting or created, was used because the data were publicly available and were inanimate financial figures. The variables, however, require further discussion. It was assumed for the study that corporate profits were important to the firm's management and to shareholders according to the philosophy within the SWM model, which contained the notion that "the firm should strive to maximize the return to shareholders" (Eiteman et al., 2007, p. 4). Market value and book value were important to corporate pricing issues because a market price that was lower than the firm's book price was assumed to indicate an underpriced security that was appropriate for inclusion in an investment portfolio to earn greater profits for shareholders (Bodie, Kane, & Marcus, 2005, p. 291; Shim et al., 1994, p. 150).

Johnstone (2007) noted that the use of the CAPM was not always appropriate because that use only addressed certain cases of pricing, due to unadjusted currency, because the units of currency varied significantly between *ex ante* and *ex post* valuation (p. 159). A similar observation was noted elsewhere in the literature concerning the use of traditional pricing techniques (Grauer, 2008, p. 150), and in certain circumstances regarding equity pricing, the "price to book value is the best standalone price multiple" (Sehgal & Pandey, 2010, p. 68). To expand upon finance theory, regarding the pricing of financial instruments from domestic companies, the study was a variation of and expansion upon the three-factor, Fama-French, multiple regression technique already in accepted use (Mirza & Afzal, 2011, p. 173).

The two independent variables of market value and book value were combined into one moderating variable (Creswell, 2009, p. 50) so that it was appropriate to use a *t*-test to look for relationships between the serialized groups of data: one independent variable, which was constructed for this study, and one dependent variable (Creswell, 2009, p. 153).

Scope and Delimitations

Because the data collected were from the public domain, single stage sampling was used to collect the data and a random sample was recommended because "with randomization, a representative sample from a population provides the ability to generalize to a population" (Creswell, 2009, p. 148). The data involved only one stratum because all of the data collected came from the same type of the previously discussed, publicly-traded U.S. electric utility companies. Instead of tables to assure random selection of companies for data collection, a computerized random number generator was employed. One means of performing this function was the serialization of the entire population of the 160 publicly-traded U.S. electric utility companies in an Excel spreadsheet and the use of an Excel random number generator to ensure the randomness of the selection of the 16 company sample. The use of the computer program Excel was not the only part of this study's analyses, but those calculations were found in similar studies (Shelor & Wright, 2011, p. 6). The size of this study's sample, only 16 companies, was found to be an insufficient amount of data to support a study involving investor withdrawals – it was assumed that there would be no withdrawals of capital invested in the sample securities for this study (Pfau, 2012, p. 36).

The purpose of this quantitative study was to analyze a sample of 16 publicly-traded U.S. electric utility companies and to extrapolate the study's results, via generalization, to the population of 160 publicly-traded U.S. electric utility companies (Creswell, 2009, p. 148). A survey instrument was not used because the firms' data were collected from the public domain. The purpose for the collection of data from the public domain was that these data were the same audited data provided to potential investors, thus making it available to anyone who may become an eventual end-user: entities such as individual investors, financial intermediaries, and portfolio managers. The data collection was cross-sectional in that the data were collected all at once. The collection method was "structured record reviews to collect financial…information" (Creswell, 2009, p. 146).

A financial records review for the years 2010, 2011, and 2012 was performed because the costs of collection were negligible or nonexistent; the data were public domain and available to anyone for potential analysis, and it was convenient for any potential researcher to confirm and verify the results from the dissertation manuscript (DM). The use of the research design in this study was a variant of the three-factor, Fama-French, multiple regression technique already in accepted use (Mirza & Afzal, 2011, p. 173). The reason that annual data for 3 years were collected in this study was that the risk *beta* for the CAPM part of the study concerned equity securities, representative of the electric utility companies in the sample of this study, and the period for the collection of those monthly data was shown to be 3 years of data when examining price changes of individual securities (Shelor & Wright, 2011, p. 4).

There were found to be different varieties of the over 3,273 electric utility companies in the United States (McNerney, 2007, para. 2) and publicly-traded U.S. electric utility companies were chosen as the study's population for several reasons. U.S. consumers rely upon electrically generated power and such "investor-owned utilities...help [to] maintain the infrastructure for the public sector" (McGowan, 2011, para. 1). "Investor-owned utilities are vital to the infrastructure of the country" (McGowan, 2011, para. 3). Publicly-traded U.S. electric utility companies were found to comprise 6% of all U.S. electric companies, had 38% of the total generating capacity, and served 71% of the U.S. public (McNerney, 2007, para. 15).

Furthermore, of the 210 of such companies, the ones that provided access to their data (reporting to the Securities and Exchange Commission [SEC]) were of the publicly-traded variety-160 of the 210, the others were privately held so that there was no access to those financials)(McNerney, 2007, paras 15-16). From an effect-size and power determination using G-Power 3.0.10 (a statistics software program-please see Appendix C), using a correlation, point biserial model, a representative sample for a *t*-test correlation study to then later extrapolate to the population by one order of magnitude (Creswell, 2009, p. 148) was a 16 company sample from the population of those 160 publicly reporting companies. The selection was within the parameters necessary achieving an input power of 0.95 and a large effect size of 0.7071068 with an actual power for the study of 0.960221.

Limitations

There were two independent variables, which were more commonly known as market value and book value. The fair market value data variable was the per share amount evaluation by the public marketplace of what the equity was worth concerning a publicly-traded company (Stickney & Weil, 2003, p. 899). The book value, in this case the book value per share of common stock (diluted–please see Appendix A), was the compilation of asset valuation by *accounting standards* so that the resulting amount determined by subtracting liabilities from assets, or the resulting equity, was then divided by the number of shares outstanding arriving at the figure for the second independent variable (Stickney & Weil, 2003, p. 875). The dependent variable was the ROA variable. ROA was useful in portfolio theory because the ROA was the "net income plus after-tax interest charges plus minority interest income divided by average total assets; perhaps the single most useful ratio for assessing management's overall operating performance" (Stickney & Weil, 2003, p. 935). The two independent variables of market value and book value were combined into one moderating variable (Creswell, 2009, p. 50) so that it was appropriate to use a *t*-test to look for relationships between the serialized groups of data: one independent variable, which was constructed for this study, and one dependent variable (Creswell, 2009, p. 153).

The first variable, which was an independent variable, was the earnings assessment, or market price, of the company's market value. The second variable, also an independent variable, was a nonearnings accounting assessment because it was the book value, or price per share (diluted), of the security. When these two variables were coupled into a ratio, the result amounted to a number less than, equal to, or greater than one. The reason for coupling these two variables was to develop an easily seen relationship between the notional, or book price of the security, and the perceived value placed upon the security by the marketplace's perception of that security. The third variable was the dependent variable because the answers to the two previous variables determined the answer to this third variable (MVBV).

Market Price 1

The fair market price data variable was the per share amount evaluation by the public marketplace of what the equity was worth concerning a publicly-traded company (Stickney & Weil, 2003, p. 899). The variable was from the ratio scale because the numbers were financial data from the New York Stock Exchange (NYSE) ending share prices for the corporate security in question (typically December 31st). The range was in U.S. dollars from zero to hundreds of dollars.

Book Value 2

The book price data variable, in this case the book value per share of common stock, was the compilation of asset valuation by accounting standards so that the resulting amount determined by subtracting liabilities from assets, or the resulting equity, was then divided by the number of shares outstanding to arrive at the figure for the second independent variable (Stickney & Weil, 2003, p. 875). The variable was from the ratio scale since the numbers were financial data from the EDGAR database provided by the SEC online derived from company financial reports. The range was in U.S. dollars from zero to hundreds of dollars.

Return-on-Assets 3

The dependent variable was the ROA variable. ROA was useful in portfolio theory because the ROA was the "net income plus after-tax interest charges plus minority interest income divided by average total assets; perhaps the single most useful ratio for assessing management's overall operating performance" (Stickney & Weil, 2003, p. 935). The two independent variables of market price and book price were combined into one moderating variable (Creswell, 2009, p. 50) so that it was appropriate to use a *t*-test to look for relationships between the serialized groups of data: one independent variable, which was constructed for this study, and one dependent variable (Creswell, 2009, p. 153). The range was in U.S. dollars from zero to hundreds of dollars divided by U.S. dollars from zero to hundreds of dollars resulting in a percentage figure.

Nontraditional, Relative Firm Price 4

The moderating variable of MVBV became the nontraditional, relative firm price variable for each of the publicly-traded U.S. electric utility companies in the 16 company sample. The NTRFV variable was a ratio numerical variable in that each of the 16 companies in the sample was determined to be, as a result of the study's analysis, either over- or underpriced.

Computer Model Variant of Company Pricing 5

The use of the study-based Excel computer model process used the Fama-French regression equation variant to devise a j-index. The j-index was mathematically a residual rectifier that in effect balanced the Fama-French regression equation's results and the residual rectifier j-index was a ratio-scale real number (a single or double digit that was either positive or negative). The j-index was depicted mathematically as a percentage and, to be of value, generally required simultaneous presentation with an explanatory mathematical set theory equivalent for each company to establish a basis for computation efficiency and effectiveness and to convey an accurate meaning for the computational result.

Company Market Capitalization 6

Although market capitalization has been generally considered by financial analysts in the common marketplace to be a ratio-scale variable in dollars, to make the MANCOVA a workable statistical analysis in this study, the ratio-scale data required conversion. The ratio-scale market capitalization for each company in the 16 company sample of publicly-traded U.S. electric utility companies was converted to a categorical variable in the following manner (please see Appendix A). If a sample firm's

market capitalization was found to be equal to or less than 1 billion dollars (U.S.), then

the firm was listed as a small capitalization company (Small Cap) and the data point was

represented by a "1." If the market capitalization of a sample firm was found to be greater

than 1 billion dollars (U.S.), but less than 5 billion dollars (U.S.), then the firm was listed

as a medium capitalization company (Medium Cap) and the data point was represented

by a "2." If the market capitalization of a sample firm was found to be equal to, or

greater than 5 billion dollars (U.S.), then the firm was listed as a large capitalization

company (Large Cap) and the data point was represented by a "3."

The Significance of the Study

Investors invested an initial investment in publicly-traded common stock and

expected the eventual recovery of the initial investment, which was not the case when the

companies underlying the purchased securities were delisted from securities exchanges

(Armstrong et al., 2011, p. 52). Investors lost their initial investment, and the profits

associated with investment securities, even though investors expected an initial

investment to be repaid along with an investment profit for an expected return (Haymore,

2011, p. 1312). A refinement of the specific problem was the analysis of publicly traded

U.S. electric utility companies' data because such utilities were integral to the U.S.

economy (McGowan, 2011, para. 3).

Publicly-traded electric utility companies were chosen as the population for this

study because this particular type of electric company generated the electricity consumed by approximately three out of four people in the United States (McNerney, 2007, para. 15). Electricity in the United States was found to be integral to the maintenance of the nation's infrastructure for the public sector and the loss of the generating capacity provided by publicly-traded U.S. electric utility companies would be catastrophic to the nation (McGowan, 2011, para. 3).

Many publicly-traded U.S. firms have a debt-ratio of between 30 and 60 % (Eiteman et al., 2007, p. 434) and U.S. firms reported a cumulative debt-ratio of 50 % (Arends, 2010, para. 10). However, when financial analysts read the parenthetical notes on balance sheets and accounted for the debt reported off-balance sheet by these same firms, the debt-ratio became 80% (Arends, 2010, para 1, 6).

The use of the creation of synthetic assets created a positive cash-flow (Chang, 2009, p. 34) such that derivative-induced assets were created (Chang, 2009, pp. 31-32) to use projected financials for firm valuation. The synthetic assets were subtracted from off-balance sheet debt to reduce the firm's debt-ratio back to the 50% figure actually reported, or the derivatives could have been used as portfolio insurance to inoculate the firm, thereby protecting the firm from a drop in asset value. The derivatives delivered principal when assets dropped, which became capital infused into a firm's balance sheet to reduce the debt-ratio back to the reported 50 % guideline. This innovation was critical to the second-stage of this study such that this procedure allowed the movement and partial recasting of a firm's financial statements. The firm valuation changed from overleveraged back to moderately leveraged at 50 % so that the firm's security would also be a purchase opportunity for prudent, potential investors. These proofs were the second stage of some of this study and hinged upon the results of the first stage wherein *t*-test correlations and regression analyses were conducted regarding the variables of market value, book value and ROA. This study's results and conclusions hold the potential to positively and constructively affect social change. Millions of investors have the opportunity to use the study's tools to mitigate or minimize losses concerning publicly-traded securities and the accompanying securities' returns may more closely mirror the investors' expected returns.

Summary

The earning of an economic profit meant that a sample publicly-traded U.S. electric utility company made profits that were above and beyond the company's basic cost of capital, known as EVA, which resulted in higher future company profitability. The general problem was that investors invested an initial investment in publicly-traded common stock and expected the eventual recovery of the initial investment, which was not the case when the companies underlying the purchased securities were delisted from securities exchanges (Armstrong et al., 2011, p. 52). The specific problem was that investors lost their initial investment, and the profits associated with investment securities, even though investors expected an initial investment to be repaid along with an investment profit for an expected return (Haymore, 2011, p. 1312). It was assumed for this study that corporate profits were important to the firm's management and to shareholders according to the philosophy contained within the SWM model, which included the notion that the firm should maximize the return to shareholders. Market value and book value were important to corporate valuation issues because a market value that was lower than the book value was assumed to indicate an undervalued security that might be appropriate for inclusion in an investment portfolio to earn greater profits for shareholders. Objective accounting measures were used, instead of just the rote, traditional finance formulae such as the CAPM and ratios, because the individual risky assets or securities were valued *ex ante* in the same monetary units in which their values were realized *ex post*. It has been commonplace for investigators to use accounting measures, such as ROA, in the evaluation of corporate performance, which helped to determine corporate valuation, and that the use of such accounting measures was still valid. To expand upon finance theory, regarding the valuation of financial instruments from domestic companies, this study was a variation of and expansion upon the three-factor, Fama-French, multiple regression technique already in accepted use. These observations were addressed in more detail in the literature review section that follows.

Chapter 2: Literature Review

Introduction

The intent of the study was to determine a means of relative (Damodaran, 2006, p. 15) firm valuation and securities repricing for all investors. The repricing was accomplished by examining the relationship between any combination of firm valuation variables using market value, book value and ROA (Chou et al., 2009, p. 193). The examination enabled the finding of high market-to-book value (Shim et al., 1994, p. 150), publicly-traded U.S. electric utility companies in a manner different from traditional techniques for such electric company valuation (Wang, 2008, p. 546). Such high market-to-book value companies found through this study allowed the use of a study-based Excel computer model process to be used with derivatives (Gubler, 2011, p. 97), to reorient those companies' debt-ratios because the amount of company debt has been shown to directly bear upon short-term performance and returns (Ozel, 2010, p. i). This short-term business revaluation intercession was the impetus necessary to eliminate investor satiation and promote an investors' resurgence of capital direct investment in those companies (Rondinelli & Burpitt, 2000, p. 181). Once investor capital movement has reoriented the company to a low market-to-book value company, then the need for the synthetic assets would have been eliminated and the derivative positions could be closed. The theory above has larger societal applications for the evaluation of all securities (inferential) in the marketplace with regard to firm revaluation, repricing of the associated securities, and the prospective inclusion of those securities in a private investor or institutional investment portfolio.

In the review of the literature, I focused upon the scholarly writings of Markowitz's of modern portfolio theory (MPT). I addressed the topics that directly related to this study involving financial economics, relative pricing and valuation, prior research, the study's control variables, related theories, propositions and models, synthetic assets, gaps in the research to the present, electric utility companies, and a summary.

Historical Research on Financial Economics

Modern Portfolio Theory Overview

The MPT was created by Markowitz in 1952. MPT deals with efficient portfolios of securities concerning those securities' "risk & return, expected return, measures of risk and volatility, and diversification" (Mangram, 2013, p. 59). According to Markowitz, the covariances associated with the number of securities, and their resulting diversification of a securities portfolio, did matter with respect to an efficient portfolio of securities (p. 60). I used MPT as a framework for this study because one of the assumptions for this study was that companies appropriate for securities investment should be part of an efficient securities portfolio and a securities covariance study was performed as a part of one of the micro-studies during this study.

MPT can be used to explain securities portfolios with the help of factors (Grinold, 2011, p. 15). There are three traditional types of portfolios: a portfolio for analysis or the portfolio of securities already owned, a portfolio associated with a certain factor (or factors) that will be examined or the target portfolio, and the portfolio that includes the factors that helped to explain the associations between the owned portfolio and the target portfolio (Grinold, 2011, p. 15). It is possible to work forward or backward from these traditional portfolios to examine expectations or returns or both (Grinold, 2011, p. 15); observations and a set of tools that were critical to this study. The data collected for the company samples were backward-looking, or the 3 previous years of information from publicly available financial statements and securities prices, and the forward look involved a prospective change to a security's price with the addition of a synthetic asset. The value of the underlying company was also updated to reflect the actual leverage as opposed to the leverage reported publicly.

The fourth portfolio was a nontraditional, hypothetical, explanatory sort of portfolio known as a "factor-mimicking portfolio" (Grinold, 2011, p. 16). The mimicking portfolio is important to quantitative financial experimentation and research (Grinold, 2011, pp. 16-17). The concept of the mimicking factor was used in this study because synthetic derivatives were used along with the debt revaluation described above. The mimicking factor was used to construct a hypothetically-valued company with an associated hypothetically priced security that may be appropriate for inclusion in a securities investment portfolio.

Foundational Financial Economics Theory

The various tenets of MPT include the CAPM propounded by four CAPM theorists: Treynor, Sharpe, Lintner, and Mossin. Arbitrage pricing theory (APT), propounded by Ross, is further related to MPT.

Foundational Financial Economics Theory of Markowitz

Harry Markowitz promoted changes to the stock price considerations promoted in
1938 by John Burr Williams: the idea that an investor would engage in the value
maximization of future security returns was changed to discounted future expected
security returns; the notion promoted in 1939 by John Richard Hicks, that anticipated
returns included some margin for risk, was altered to the notion that the securities'
anticipated returns capitalization should "vary with risk" (Markowitz, 1952a, p. 77).
Some portfolio changes promoted by Markowitz were that portfolio elections were based
upon seven assumptions: efficient portfolios needed to be determined and an optimal
portfolio was chosen from the set of efficient portfolios; the optimal portfolios were
contained within the three-dimensional space inside the area of a graph of multiple
functions.

Markowitz's seven assumptions. Changes made by Markowitz to portfolio theory
portfolio choices accepted at that time were based upon the acceptance of seven
assumptions. The first assumption was that investors were rational because Markowitz
believed that investors expected investments to accumulate high returns and those returns
should be "stable" [and] "certain" (Markowitz, 1959, p. 6). The second assumption was
that investors cared nothing for risk (Markowitz, 1952a, p. 91). The third was that the
investor's consumption function was a naturally increasing function (Markowitz, 1952b,
p. 151). The fourth was that the securities investment model's analysis was based upon a

single time period (Markowitz, 1959, p. 299).

The fifth assumption was that the utility graph had breaks, in which the optimal curve was depicted to be increasing and concave concerning an investor's needs for consumption and the investor's rationality concerning risk aversion and, therefore, implied that the investor's needs curve was not an unbroken concave function (Markowitz, 1959, p. 296). The utility curve was a continuous, smooth function, that contained two orders of derivatives, such that the function occupied the first quadrant and the function was a rising, upward, serpentine, "continuous curve" (Markowitz, 1952b, p. 151).

The sixth assumption was that an investor, in light of the conceivable portfolios extant, might pick a return rate such that the expected securities return could increase as a result of increasing the portfolio's variance or the portfolio's variance could be reduced and the reduced variance would result in the portfolio's loss of expected returns (Markowitz, 1952a, p. 79). Therefore, if "E" equaled expected return and if "V" equaled variance (or risk), the investor would accept a minimal variance (or risk) for a given portfolio's expected return and the same investor would further accept a "maximum E for [a] given V or less" (Markowitz, 1952a , p. 82). The seventh assumption was that when the returns variability of a certain portfolio was based upon risk; more efficient portfolios would result from semivariance calculations because variance analysis eliminated the extreme, statistical outliers whereas semivariance analysis was based upon "reducing losses" (Markowitz, 1959, p. 194).

Decisions regarding efficient securities portfolios.

Concerning the set of efficient securities portfolios that existed from which a potential investor could possibly choose, Markowitz noted that several decisions should be made (Markowitz, 1952a, pp. 78-79). If the portfolio to be chosen were a vector such that each probable portfolio security is the fraction of the overall portfolio invested in each prospective security, such that each security is actually a covariance matrix, the chain equation inputs would then be the "matrix of covariances…[the] vector of expected returns…[the resulting] *A*, an *m* by *n* matrix…[and] *b*, an *m* element vector" (Markowitz, 1959, pp. 170-172).

The first decision to be made, according to Markowitz (1959), was that the efficient set of portfolios needed to be determined, because of the implication, for V (meaning variance) and E (meaning expected returns), because "there exists a portfolio which maximizes E" [and thus, by default, there would also be such a portfolio that minimizes V] (Markowitz, 1959, p. 177). The second decision, after determination of the efficient set of portfolios because not all variance was eliminated by the use of portfolio diversification (Markowitz, 1952a, p. 79), was that a choice should be made from that set of efficient portfolios the optimal portfolio by increasing and decreasing the amounts and numbers of securities in the portfolio through the use of "formal computations" (Markowitz, 1952a, p. 91).

Isolating efficient portfolios to maximize return and minimize risk.

Markowitz, in choosing the portfolios from the efficient set that maximize return and minimize risk, related to the optimization discussion of portfolio selection by a prospective investor. When the efficient portfolios were determined, not all securities in the set chosen would be part of the set of efficient portfolios and not all asset classes would be represented in an efficient portfolio made up of only a part of the conceivable securities choices (Markowitz, 1959, p. 26). When the potential securities of an optimal, efficient portfolio were considered, the points on the graph of the various securities combinations where the function suddenly changed directions were all efficient portfolios and were known as "corner portfolios" (Markowitz, 1959, p. 24).

With a perceived optimal portfolio, the optimal portfolio choice for a given moment in time for an investor occurred at the point of intersection of several curves or lines. The optimal investor's portfolio occurred where the "isomean curve" (Markowitz, 1952a, p. 84) (all portfolios with a particular expected return) crossed the "isovariance line" (p. 84) (all portfolios with a particular return variance or risk) that then crossed the efficient portfolios line, which started at the centroid of the isomean curve circles. When the three lines (or graphs) did not intersect, the subset of optimal portfolios was then contained within the three-dimensional space contained within the area of the graph where the circular curve and both of the lines were proximally tangent to each another (Markowitz, 1952a, pp. 85-86).

A summary of Markowitz's changes to modern portfolio theory.

Markowitz made changes to the security price portion of modern portfolio theory portfolio choices in the 1950s. The belief that an investor must engage in the value maximization of future security returns was changed by Markowitz to the discounting of expected future security returns. The notion that anticipated returns must include some margin for risk was changed by Markowitz claimed to the idea that the securities' anticipated returns capitalization must vary with risk. An investor could then pick a rate of return, so that the securities return expected would then increase by increasing the portfolio's variance, or pick the option that the portfolio's variance could be lessened and the variance reduction would result in the portfolio's loss of expected returns. When the returns variability of a portfolio was based upon risk, then more efficient portfolios developed from semivariance calculations because variance analysis eradicated the extreme outliers because semivariance analysis focused upon reducing portfolio losses. When the optimal, efficient portfolios were graphically considered; of the various securities combinations where the function changed direction, those points on the graph were all considered to be efficient portfolios and those critical points were all known as corner portfolios.

Historical Research on Relative Pricing and Valuation

The principal reason to pursue research in the area of revaluation and the relative pricing of securities in particular was because the practitioner models that traders used to combat investor risk aversion were useful in the theoretical pricing aspects of securities (Condie & Ganguli, 2011, p. 231). The relationships relating to return and risk of corporate securities, where the more recent data examined were free from issues associated with the market loss of companies that had become defunct and their associated securities removed from the trading exchanges, were found to be

significant (Chou et al., 2009, p. 193). According to prospect theory, "the negative risk-

return relation is driven by the mixture of risk attitudes for firms of different

performances" (Chou et al., p. 207). These findings served as a theoretical platform for

this study by using the Fama and French methodology and similar regression techniques,

confirmed applications secondary to prospect theory, and disallowed the solitary but not

the combined use with other techniques of the CAPM and prospectively APT (Chou et

al., pp. 193-194). Positive and negative relationships promoted risk and return linkages in

the use of accounting data for corporate security accounting measures of return, namely

ROA and comparisons to measures of central tendency such as outliers to the mean, in a

way very similar to this study (Chou et al., pp. 193-194).

Various accounting measures for firms were found to have mathematical

relationships and were related to types of returns in a non-traditional, relative valuation

way (Damodaran, 2007, p. 44). The findings of Damodaran (2007) were important to this

study because accounting variables were used in a theoretical way, conducive to stages

one and two of this study concerning the analysis of some hypothetical constructs. The

findings related to developed material cogent to stage two of this study in that returns

were tied to non-traditional, relative corporate valuation, and standard industrial

classification (SIC) returns were benchmarked by segmentation of industries for

comparison (p. 66).

The use of the findings of Damodaran (2006) provided an evidentiary and theoretical platform for further study concerning the measurements associated

with valuation and the different approaches to the methods for corporate security

valuation. For example, a variety of forms of regression, mathematical methods

evaluations, samples for different types of industries, and comparisons of methods and

solutions were supported by the literature and mathematical proofs (pp. 28-30). One

finding was that the regression of book value, a variable in this study, and revenue, a

value critical to market value, another variable in this study, "have higher explanatory

power than the regressions for price earnings ratios" (p. 72). The findings of Damodaran

(2006) were important to this study because a platform for further study was provided for

non-traditional, relative valuation, repricing, and the methods framework for this study

(p. 2). The findings established that valuation and the associated relative pricing, the

topics of this study, were critical to finance (p. 2). The findings of Damodaran (2006)

were a part of the theoretical research platform to support this study.

Non-traditional, relative valuation techniques, instead of traditional finance

formulae, were used to determine "realistic valuation" (Fernandez, 2007, p. 13) of

corporate securities in some of the Standard and Poor's 500 (S&P 500) index of

companies. The analytical treatment methodologies performed by the investigator in

Fernandez (2007) were various correlation coefficient examinations and analyses of how

the debt and equity of those companies examined had increased over the data array period

for those 271 companies analyzed for a data sample period of 14 years. Some of the

variables were market values, book values of the debt and equity, and specifically how those variables related to movements in the debt-ratios of the 271 companies

over the 14-year period. This methodology and the associated techniques, along with a

number of similar variables used, were a method of theoretical investigation, and a

platform of study, similar to this study. That study was relevant to this study because of

the demonstration that it was possible to mathematically, via equation substitution (p.

14), and empirically, via non-traditional, relative valuation (p. 16) and re-pricing, to show

that book value, a variable in this study, and market value, another variable in this study,

have a relationship to returns (p. 13); some relationships were negative and others were

positive. The main consideration for the use of non-traditional relative book revaluation

of the underlying firm and the relative prospective repricing of the associated firm's

securities was that the use of earnings was inconsistent since earnings quality varied with

"business cycles and macroeconomic variables" (Kim & Qi, 2010, p. 937). These

considerations were vital to the conduct of this study since the variables, along with the

methodology utilized, were critical to the conduct of the two stages of this study

concerning some of the hypothetical constructs.

An important consideration of this study was that the use of models was

important, but was not the complete study. Securities analysts noted that the market price

of a security, compared with the range of prices for that security historically, was the

significant factor that supported analysts' recommendations of the security; two-thirds of

analysts did not support the EMH and one-third contended that the CAPM was not

significant in predicting security prices (Mukherji & Youngho, 2013, p. 46).

The various types of measures to assess financial performance of the firm and the firm's accompanying financial instruments have been discussed, explained, and verified (Gentry & Shen, 2010, p. 520). For two sets of constructs, the first stage of this study involved the use of correlation coefficients, to establish a positive or negative relationship between the various measures, and the second stage was used as a verification, or confirmation step, to aid in the establishment of a causal relationship by using several forms of regression studies (p. 522). There has been a continuing debate among scholars concerning the relationship between the measures of firm performance and the resulting performance of the associated securities of those firms examined; a medium positive correlation for a variety of industries within an industry has been confirmed (p. 522). The findings mentioned were relevant to this study because the methodology used by the investigators in Gentry and Shen (2010), which was a two-pronged approach of a correlation study and a confirming set of regression studies, was the same and provided the methodological and theoretical platform for this study. Similar to this study, the Gentry and Shen (2010) findings provided a platform for the study of relationships between an accounting measure of firm profitability, such as book value, and a market measure of firm profitability, such as market value, along with the creation of a moderating variable, such as MVBV. Furthermore, the investigators in Gentry and Shen (2010) compared those analyzed variables' findings with the short term accounting measure of profitability known as ROA; similar to this study.

The author of Ozel (2010) ascertained how rational economic agents functioned in the open economy, concerning initial investment in a firm's securities, and whether there was information asymmetry associated with investors' choices concerning differences between the choices involving corporate debt and how potential investors evaluated that debt; corporate cash flow or corporate earnings (p. 1). Four variable constructs were intended for use, but the investigator in the study used proxies such as MVBV and market returns to plug data for the intended variables, similar to this study.

For corporate debt with regard to potential direct investment in the firm's securities by potential investors, company earnings secondary to market returns was an important consideration for potential investors. The other finding was that information asymmetry was significant to the determinations made by potential investors to make initial direct investment in firm securities because those investors had better information than the public. This resource was important to this study because it set the theoretical platform for the various stage two parts of this study for two sets of constructs, which change the debt-ratio of a firm to decrease firm leverage so that the reduction in the firm's debt increases investor direct initial investment in the associated firm's securities.

Review of Prior Research

Introduction

In each part of the following literature review, the following six questions were answered where appropriate and applicable in order to complete the transition for each part from discussion initiation to study applicability: what was the subject area; how did the subject area relate to financial economics; what was the origin of the subject area;

who were the contributors to the subject area with a bearing upon this study; what did those contributions mean; and how did the subject area apply to this study? The subject areas that were discussed in the following literature review were: this study's control variables; modern portfolio theory; agency theory; prospect theory; extreme value theory (EVT); efficient market theory (EMT); the shareholder wealth maximization model (SWM); impaired assets; investor satiation; synthetic assets; the CAPM; the Carhart four-factor model; the Fama-French three-factor model; gaps in research and electric utility companies; risk; and a summary.

This Study's Control Variables

The study's control variables were company security risk *beta* (Khan, 2012, p. 193), the proxy for investor satiation of company market capitalization (Kopelman, 2010, p. 5), and company assets impairment (Guni & Negurita, 2011, p. 975).

Company Security Risk *Beta*

This study involved the calculation of the prospective return of individual securities and for individual securities the association between a security's return and the security's risk *beta* was found to be a cornerstone of the Field of Finance (Shelor & Wright, 2011, p. 6). The calculation of *beta* using the CAPM and the computer program Excel were not the only part of this study's analyses, but those calculations were found in similar studies to be an important part of those studies (p. 4). In working with the debt of a firm, the cost of equity was found to be important and over 80 percent of advisors who practiced finance were found to use the CAPM and *beta* to help determine firm equity (and by default, the prospective value and pricing of those firm equity securities) (Mukherji & Youngho, 2013, p. 48). A firm's size (market capitalization) and equity shown by a market-to-book variable were both variables shown to be market priced based so that the market price of a firm's equity security and its prospective return were important to this study (Morelli, 2012, p. 47).

Regarding the relevance to finance, to minimize test bias, improve the power of the test, and to be able to use smaller sample sizes of individual securities under examination, it was found that a cross-sectional regression (CSR) version of the Fama and French three-factor model in some of the second of two stages was appropriate (using some assigned *betas*), depending upon whether the data collected was found to be statistically normally or non-normally distributed (Kim & Qi, 2010, p. 939).

Based upon the results of previous studies, it was found that the results of this study mirrored those previous study results such that the expected returns of the individual securities were positively correlated relative to the security *betas*; this was not known until the data was collected and analyzed (Mukherji & Youngho, 2013, p. 52). The reason that the test *betas* and the test portfolio data plug information was collected from the Fama and French data website, and from the EDGAR database regarding market pricing of individual securities, was that previous studies have shown that data collection from such acknowledged information service websites was an effective method for the gathering and then the effective eventual analysis of such data (Mcdonald, Michelfelder, & Theodossiou, 2010, p. 375).

The Proxy for Investor Satiation

A researcher noted that 70 percent of the trades on the New York Stock Exchange were conducted by institutions, so the market's reaction to the pricing of a firm's securities was essentially found to be an institutional response to the market and trading activities (Balog, 1975, p. 84). Recent findings from the print news media demonstrated that currently 88 percent of all equity market trades were made by institutional and professional fund traders, as well as by high-frequency computer trades that made up 56 percent of all trades, as opposed to only 11 percent of all trades being made by retail or consumer types of private traders (Editorial, 2011, para. 4). Therefore, in order to appeal to the market, a security's market price must appeal to institutions and high-frequency computer trading algorithms.

A basic definition of investor satiation was found to be that a publicly listed firm's market capitalization was the size of that firm's market capitalization (Wang, Chen, & Cheng, 2011, p. 143); investors were sated with the level of purchases of that particular security as demonstrated by the amounts already purchased. A publicly listed firm's market capitalization was used as a proxy for investor satiation in this study because it was found to be the case from examinations, of the over 100 Fama and French portfolios in use for publicly traded securities' examination by analysts, that market capitalization size was already useful as a proxy (Wei, Qianqiu, Rhee, & Liang, 2010, p. 156).

Theorists originally noted that conglomerate mergers were, from the firm perspective, the best use of capital and that managers only undertook a conglomerate merger in order to more effectively augment or control capital and that the firm's shareholders encouraged this sort of managerial activity to promote value creation (Shapiro, 1970, p. 643). However, it was recently found that two *ex ante* important factors for the examination of publicly listed corporate securities were capital structure (the amount of corporate debt leverage) and company size (market capitalization) (Bhalla, 2011, p. 20). The amount of company debt and a firm's market capitalization, the proxy for investor satiation, were both important to this study.

Firm Assets Impairment

It was shown, for the recent four decade period, that the 1,000 largest firms in the United States have steadily decreased the correlation between current revenues and current expenses such that there was an increasing correlation during that period between current period revenue and the expenses from periods occurring before and after the revenue period depicted in the financial statements (Donelson, Jennings, & McInnis, 2011, p. 945). This observation has been demonstrated in the improper reporting of corporate debt in financial statements (Arends, 2010, para. 10). Since expensing was found to be associated with debt (Donelson, Jennings, & McInnis, 2011, p. 963), and debt was an issue in this study, and the write-down of impaired assets was an accepted accounting protocol (p. 963), the consideration of impaired assets (along with debt) was an important factor for study in this study.

Although the Federal Accounting Standards Board issued SFAS 121 (*Accounting for the Impairment of Long-Lived Assets)* in order to provide guidance for firms

to properly account for the impairment of long-term assets, firms have failed overall to

properly account for the lost value associated with the impairment of long-term assets,

which was part of the rationale for this study (Riedl, 2002, p. iii). It has been shown that

debt with risk was nominally shown to effectively imbue a firm with what amounts to a

derivative put option, which then was shown to involve the dissipation of the returns on

physical assets such as the long-term assets of a firm (Beaver & Ryan, 2009, p. 2). Since

the use of a derivative commonality has already been demonstrated, it was just a

common-sense application of the same theoretical application to temporarily reverse a

firm's debt structure with the frictionless derivative payouts of synthetic assets (Gubler,

2011, pp. 68 & 97) to affect a revalution of the underlying firm and a repricing of the

associated firm's equity securities.

The use of depreciation by a firm was actually shown to overturn the results of

Miller and Modligliani proposition tenets (Dammon & Senbet, 2012, p. 358) and the

depreciated long-term assets of a firm that were also impaired was reflected as a

percentage in the calculations during the data analysis phase of this study since

depreciation was shown to affect a firm's debt (p. 358). Depreciation and by default asset

impairment were (relatively speaking) already shown to be a percentage of the original

fair market value calculation equations of a long-term asset's valuation (p. 360).

Concerning symmetry, with regard to the Field of Accounting, depreciation and by

default asset impairment have been considered unifying factors in the financial statements for all firms (p. 360).

Agency Theory

It was noted in the literature that agency theory originated in 1976 with the publication of Jensen and Meckling's study results on firm theory and that agents, who were managers of the firm, could influence the economic results of the firm with managerial actions (Bryant & Davis, 2012, p. 3). Since it was conclusively shown that agency problems occur when firm managers improve their compensation or benefits by violating agency trust in sacrificing the interests of the stockholders (Xian, Chen, & Moldousupova, 2011, p. 123), one of the assumptions for this study was that managers act on behalf of the firm's principals. Another way of looking at this concept was derived from the literature in that the principal in the principal-agent relationship was indeed not even actually the shareholders of the firm but was in fact the corporation itself (Lan & Heracleous, 2010, p. 294).

Agency theory, with regard to corporate finance, was found to be the limitation of company managers' *ex post* behavior, which would tend to reduce future decisions' *ex ante* costs, in that managers were supposed to act on behalf of a firm's shareholders (maximizing value for those firm owners) in light of the "usual frictions-taxes, bankruptcy costs, agency costs, and asymmetric information" (Boot & Thakor, 2011, p. 3436). Firm market values were shown to increase as the managers of a firm increasingly assumed more debt to finance firm growth projects (Umutlu, 2010, p. 1005). The factors that prevented firms from being 100 percent leveraged with debt, which was coincidentally a consideration that resulted in a firm's capital structure being balanced between debt and equity and thus the firm to be considered optimally structured or optimized, were the agency considerations of "bankruptcy costs, asymmetric information and agency costs" (p. 1006). The second consideration from modern agency theory was that the board of directors was no longer an agent of the shareholders but that the board was a stand-alone entity that was empowered to act on behalf of beneficiaries; in this case that the corporation would again be the principal and that the board would not monitor executive officers of the firm but would instead mediate the claims from all concerned stakeholders as a "mediating hierarch" (Lan & Heracleous, 2010, p. 295).

One of the assumptions of this study was that general and total bankruptcy would be averted long before the firm would be in danger of such bankruptcy because of a firm manager's common sense attribute of self-preservation; managerial compensation would generally cease when the firm ceased to exist. Another assumption was that a firm manager would signal to the public, since the manager had asymmetric information that the public did not, with certain decisions concerning debt and equity policies since the market price of firm securities may not reflect the actual book value of a firm (Umutlu, 2010, p. 1006). This consideration was important to this study since it was intended that the sample firms' book value was to prospectively be revalued to include off-balance sheet debt and debt shown in the parenthetical notes (but not on the balance sheets) and the associated firm's securities (common shares) were repriced with synthetic derivatives and the revalued capital structure just discussed.

Another assumption of this study was that agency costs would exist regardless of a firm's capital structure and that the change in those costs would not be appreciably changed since the costing would inevitably be based upon agency costing "stale information" (Grinold, 2011, p. 26). It was assumed that there would prospectively be a profound change in a firm's book revaluation to include unrecorded debt, along with the associated prospective market change in a firm's security pricing, and that there would be no effective means for adjusting the costing frictions for the firm's new value and price; agency cost frictions and their changes were considered moot for this study (Umutlu, 2010, p. 1005).

Risk and Prospect Theory

The concept of a normal distribution of data in a graph was found to have been used for hundreds of years, but such an application to finance was shown to have started with use of a normal data distribution by Bachelier around the year 1900 (Barbieri, Dubikovsky, Gladkevich, Goldberg, & Hayes, 2010, p. 1091). An assumption of this study was that the risk associated with finance data normalcy (related to the central limit theorem) would also become attributed to being in use as of the date listed above that described such finance data normality (Barbieri et al., 2010, p. 1091). It was noted that such a use of normalcy was also associated with the modeling of price changes in stocks, which was important to this study, and that the concepts of normalcy and risk were useful to the pricing of equity options and to the modeling of risks associated with equity issues; concepts that were useful in this study (p. 1091).

49

Prospect theory (PT) was developed by Kahneman and Tversky in their 1979 study and PT was shown to be used conventionally by people who dealt with elementary issues that were easily explained (Bromiley, 2010, p. 1357). That original research and PT have evolved to include the more complicated choices made by people and the microeconomic risk issues that occur at the firm level (p. 1357). Scholars have shown that PT and risk have evolved simultaneously to become related issues when dealing with the issues just described (p. 1357); PT and risk both related to this study because the types of decision-making just described, along with the risk just discussed, were a part of this study.

There has been shown to be a great deal of economic disturbance in the marketplace since 2006 and the cause of that disturbance has been attributed to the predisposition of financial firms to assume increasing amounts of risk, whether during periods of stable finances or during periods of growth, of an economic nature (Garvey, 2010, p. 789). Although there has been a considerable amount of theoretical support for PT, and how decisions were made by individuals concerning risk-aversion, utility theory and the related traditional consumer behavior of personal consumption were shown to dominate risky decision-making present theory and the marketplace (p. 791).

An important reason for the reliance upon traditional utility theory was found to be the manner of the risk calculation of acceptance of risk in finance and it was predicated upon the relationship between the determination of the allocation of assets and the toleration of risk variables (Gilliam, Chatterjee, & Grable, 2010, p. 30); the basic measures of asset allocation and risk toleration were important to the latter

aspects of this study. It should be noted that the aversion of risk in finance was found to

be more than just a distaste by consumers for the occurrence of higher standard

deviations of security returns (Hobbs & Sharma, 2011, p. 59): risk adversity was shown

to be more than subservience to the "mean-variance framework" (p. 63). An assumption

of this study was data distribution normality, but it was shown that when return moments

of a higher nature were considered by investors that risk could be reduced and that the

expectation of returns that were non-normal or skewed could help to avert another market

anomaly such as the financial debacle that occurred in the years 2008-2009 in the U.S.

marketplace (p. 63). Studies performed previous to the 2006-2008 economic crisis have

shown that the data for utility companies was marked by a certain level of skewness and

kurtosis such that those data were considered to be non-normal in the manner of

statistical distribution and returns (Mcdonald, Michelfelder, & Theodossiou, 2010, p.

377). The data that was collected for this study was from the years 2010, 2011, and 2012;

those data were normally distributed once the data were collected and analyzed for the

dissertation manuscript (DM) by the use of one-dozen data plugs out of hundreds of data

points.

Although the traditional means for the forecasting of financial statements has

been the use of the sales percentage method, it was shown that the use of averaged

industry data could be used and defended to financial institution auditors and skeptics

(Jalbert, Briley, & Jalbert, 2012, p. 123). This consideration was important to this study because the financial data were technically updated to reflect the actual amount

of debt carried by firms, from the statistically drawn data collected in this study, and that

the firms' relevered book value, as well as the updated market price of those securities

involved the use of applied synthetic assets, will need to be credible to the financial

professionals who will examine those results (p. 124). Just like the financial data

examined by researchers, the data collected in this study will be highly credible because

those data resembled the researchers' data in that they were also: a) averages of data for

firms that have been ongoing and established; b) from a small, statistical sample of

established firms that do not include entrepreneurial or small firms just getting started; c)

from firms that have a nationwide audience such as those in this study, which have been

publicly traded U.S. electric utility companies; and d) the type of financial data that has

been publicly reported and those data have been deemed to be historical in nature (p.

128).

Extreme Value Theory (EVT)

EVT was not useful to this study based upon the sample data collected and

analyzed. EVT has to do with the eventual data distribution being normal or non-normal

and EVT would have been useful to increase study power if the data collected were found

to be non-normally distributed after the use of data plugs; EVT has to do with a more

advanced statistical evaluation of the fat tails involved with data point outliers in

potentially non-normally distributed data (if those data were processed as non-normal –

but those collected data were normalized with the use of just several data plugs)

(Balakrishnan, Davies, Keating, & Mason, 2011, p. 1074). Box-and-whiskers

plots of the data collected were the nominal step in determining the existence of such data

outliers evident in the data collected such that EVT would even be applicable for data

modeling and the forecasting of associations pertinent to those data (Gomes, Henriques-

Rodrigues, & Miranda, 2011, p. 443). As such, it was not necessary to use EVT.

Efficient Market Theory (EMT)

Efficient market theory (EMH) was found to be one of the most important tenets

of finance and a principal basis for research conducted in the Field of Financial

Economics (Condie & Ganguli, 2011, p. 230; Hodnett & Heng-Hsing, 2012, p. 849). An

examination of EMH found that EMH involved ideal conditions in the market wherein

capital markets were found to be completely efficient, all information was immediately

incorporated without information asymmetry into market pricing, investors were found to

be rational in their expectations, and investors were risk averse (Hodnett & Heng-Hsing,

2012 p. 849). Consistent with EMH, these were all assumptions in this study. EMH was

also found to be the basis for theories such as MPT and models such as the CAPM (p.

849), both of which were used in this study. Further, researchers in the current literature

realized that two sections, namely that a perfectly efficient lending market existed and

that all investors were part of an efficient market where all current prices were known

and the investors' predictions of expected values in the future were identical, were not

always consistent for investors and markets, contrary to the views of Markowitz and

Treynor (Zakamulin, 2011, p. 1).

Eugene Fama originally suggested that one of the tenets of EMH, strata involving the efficiency of capital markets, could be used as a means of dividing EMH into three different varieties of the original EMH theory: strong form, semi-strong form, and the weak form (Hodnett & Heng-Hsing, 2012, p. 850). The strong form of market efficiency included the notions that there was no inside information and that markets were perfectly efficient; the semi-strong form included the notion that all information that was universally available was included in efficient market pricing and that analysts who used fundamental tools could not outperform with better returns in such a market; and the weak form allowed that historical prices were included in market pricing such that analysts that used technical means could not improve upon returns in the weak-form efficient market (p. 850).

One of the assumptions involved with EMH was noted to be the idea that the pricing of market securities was a random matter and was unpredictable, but the use of EMH over time has resulted in the acceptance of the idea that EMH does allow for the prediction of price changes based upon the difference between the real market price of a security and the price predicted from the use of "multifactor models" (Pan, 2011, p. 201). These concepts were important to this study since real prices were part of the data collection and multifactor models were used to analyze those data.

Miller and Modigliani's Propositions I and II

Franco Modigliani and Merton Miller were collaterally involved in the development of pricing theory, as well as the practitioner models posited by primary theorists, because Modigliani and Miller recognized the support of primary

theorist Lintner regarding Propositions I and II before the CAPM was simultaneously

introduced by Lintner and various primary theorists (Modigliani & Miller, 1958, p. 261).

A primary theorist mentioned Modigliani and Miller's work after the introduction of the

CAPM (Sharpe, 1964, p. 427). Jack Treynor acknowledged that the Treynor studies of

agent reasonable and ideal behavior eventually lead to the corroboration of Modigliani

and Miller's Proposition I (MMI) (Treynor, 1962, p. 1). Modigliani and Miller's

Proposition I posited that: a) firm market value was exclusive of a firm's capital structure

and that the value was based upon the revenue rate resulting from the various classes of

that firm's equity securities (Modigliani & Miller, 1958, pp. 268-269) and b) MMI was

based upon the idea that MMI could be originated with an end goal of either the

maximization of a firm's market value or the firm's profits (p. 262).

The impetus behind the development of Propositions I and II (MMI&II) by

Modigliani and Miller was that the Field of Corporate Finance was not well served by the

macroeconomic theory posited by Keynes and Hicks and that the then current

microeconomic theory was not useful for the necessary calculations to make firms

profitable (Modigliani & Miller, 1958, p. 263). Modigliani and Miller posited the belief

that the value of an investment decision, a reason for the need for MMI&II regarding firm

capital, should not be based upon the status of firm ownership at the moment when those

decisions were made by management (p. 264). Modigliani and Miller decided that equity

position holders could liquidate their shares of firm ownership and if the shareholders disagreed with management concerning firm value or the disposition of prospective firm financial projects, those shareholders would still be able to benefit from the sale of those shares and the streams of revenue accompanying the shares up to the sale (p. 264).

Modigliani and Miller were able to determine the MMI conclusions because the two researchers allowed that the shares and share classes of like and type firms, suggestive of the Marshall equity theory, should be substitutable in financial calculations for firm valuation (Modigliani & Miller, 1958, p. 266). Therefore, Modigliani and Miller were able to: a) equalize projected future rates of return for shares in share classes that were homogeneous across related firms in a category; b) equalize the price that a prospective shareholder might be willing to pay for such shares across homogeneous classes of shares; and c) bring the analysis of bonds into the expected capitalization of the rates for homogeneous firms from the market for substitutable equities discussed earlier by considering debt as "perpetual bonds" (p. 266). By default, the incurred debt and the value of that debt in homogeneous firms did have a bearing upon homogeneous firm security pricing and the value of the associated firm under consideration (p. 268).

The rationale concerning the constructs involved with MMI&II was that, in an uncertain world and market, the associated constructs and theory could conceivably be used to value securities and the underlying firms associated with those securities (Modigliani & Miller, 1958, p. 296). MMI&II theory and the model constructs were achieved by dismissing or adapting a large number of meaningful factors for the model and the associated equations, to include but were not to be limited to: full

equilibrium in the experimental space; perfect competition; fully rational agents;

homogeneously sized firms; and the size of the obtainable market for securities and debt;

and that these and other assumptions to make the theory and model work were merely

provided as "simplifications" (p. 296). These observations were important to this study

because this study's methodology involved the relevering of a firm's debt and the

repricing of the associated firm's equity security since it was only possible for a firm to

have so much debt versus so much equity in order to remain in business. If the firm were

not in business, there would have been no data for the years 2010, 2011, and 2012 to

perform this study.

Shareholder Wealth Maximization Model (SWM)

An assumption in this study was that corporate profits were important to the

firm's management and to shareholders because the shareholder wealth maximization

(SWM) model included the notion that a firm's management should maximize

shareholder return (Eiteman et al., 2007, p. 4). Market value and book value were

important to corporate valuation issues since a market value that was lower than the book

value was assumed to indicate a low market-to-book value security that might be

appropriate for inclusion in an investment portfolio to earn greater profits for

shareholders (Shim et al., 1994, p. 150; Bodie, Kane, & Marcus, 2005, p. 291). The use

of the CAPM was not always appropriate since the use of the model only addressed

certain cases of valuation, due to unadjusted currency, because the units of currency were shown to vary significantly between *ex ante* and *ex post* valuation (Johnstone,

2007, p. 159). A similar observation was noted elsewhere in the literature concerning the

use of traditional valuation techniques (Grauer, 2008, p. 150) and, in fact, in certain

circumstances regarding equity valuation, the "price to book value is the best standalone

price multiple" (Sehgal & Pandey, 2010, p. 68). To expand upon current finance theory

regarding the valuation of financial instruments from domestic companies, this study was

a variation of, and expansion upon, the three-factor, Fama-French, multiple regression

technique already in accepted use (Mirza & Afzal, 2011, p. 173).

Synthetic Assets

Pairs-trading and the creation of synthetic assets have been disregarded for the

previous 20 years, but synthetic asset creation could and should be a viable trading

technique for portfolio theory and the practitioner management of financial portfolios

(Chang, 2009, p. 27). A significant finding was that the creation of synthetic assets, such

as the use of pairs-trading, was found to be profitable secondary to the reactions from

arbitrage-like opportunities resulting from "stock-price overreaction and lead-lag price

reaction between component stocks [of the synthetically created asset]" (p. 34). The

findings noted were relevant to this study because synthetic assets provided profitable

returns, the constraints enumerated were necessary to obtain profits from synthetic assets

in general and pairs trading in particular, and because the findings illustrated the arbitrage

conditions necessary for some synthetic asset creations to provide the potential returns

necessary to implement the stage two analyses of this study (p. 35).

The investigator in Turnbull (2009) listed and calculated the impact of issues associated with created financial instruments and used that information for "assessing, measuring and managing the risk of new products" (p. 87). There was no sample size since the article was characterized by the use of mathematical chain equations involving substitution proofs (pp. 90-91) and the use of set theory to examine the results that stemmed from the use of those proofs (p. 92). This was an important concept for understanding the operationalization of the fifth set of hypotheses constructs in this study because the method used was the same. The common-sense means of determining valuation and price was to look at the obligated payment stream, relating to the instrument within the associated financial tranche, so that the interplay between asset value, limited information to derive pricing, and the associations with cash flow would have a better explanation and relationship in theory. That study was relevant to this study because it set the theoretical foundation for the stage two analyses parts of this study wherein a contrived, financial instrument was created to change the debt ratio and valuation of a firm to induce initial direct investor investment in corporate securities.

The creation and use of synthetic assets was found to be important to this study because it was found to be one of the four parts of academic and professional practice in the Field of Finance (Pan, 2011, pp. 197-198). Although it was previously believed that the use of synthetic assets would yield a return similar to that of the use of risk-free assets, it was found that in higher volatility markets that the sales of certain derivatives, for example, of "zero-beta straddles" (Ang, Goetzmann, & Schaefer, 2010, p. 193) resulted in a positive, back-tested return on securities of approximately three percent every week (p. 193). These observations were important because a volatile market was an assumption for this study and the use of synthetic assets and derivatives helped to revalue the underlying firm and to reprice the associated securities for analysis in this study.

Capital Asset Pricing Model

Pricing models such as the CAPM evolved from capital market theories, such as the EMH, which were associated with the capital markets in general (Hodnett & Heng-Hsing, 2012, p. 849). Eugene Fama and Kenneth French, by using a three-factor model that used the factors of market-to-book ratio, the size of the company (or market capitalization), and market risk, were able to account for "95% of the variability in stock returns" (Pan, 2011, p. 201). The CAPM was found to be appropriate in the study of capital costing, some debt considerations and the return on capital for publicly held U.S. electric utility companies by state commissions that monitor such utilities, the courts, and federal agencies (Mcdonald, Michelfelder, & Theodossiou, 2010, p. 375). There were some primary theorists concerning the CAPM, which follow, who bear mentioning since the CAPM was used for a part of this study's methodology.

Jack Treynor as a CAPM Primary Theorist

Jack Treynor posited the "Theory of Market Value of Risky Assets" (Treynor, 1962, p. 1) and assumptions that increased the modern portfolio theory work of Markowitz (p. 2). Treynor's market value theory assumptions were that: a) there were no taxes; b) there were no transactional expense costs; c) individual investor securities purchases were insignificant resulting in no effect upon prices; d) with relation to first and second results derivatives, "investors maximize[d] expected utility" (p. 2); e) investors were risk averse, similar to Markowitz' second assumption; f) there was a perfectly efficient lending market; and g) an efficient market included all investors such that all current prices were known *and* the investors' expected values of securities in the future were the same (p. 2).

Treynor separated the prospective investors' projected, expected, security returns into two, cumulative-resultant parts (Treynor, 1962, p. 5). The initial part of the security return: a) no matter how the investor invested, the rate of return of capital was calculated from the use of the risk-free rate of lending and was added to the second part; and b) the expected return based upon the assumed risk for any taken risks and those taken risks had no relationship to the originally invested capital (p. 6).

Treynor's market value theory allowed for a separatist, theoretical viewpoint of the mathematics and the resulting rigor of those calculations. The experimental space used for consideration of the calculations was that (to make the theory work in a limited way) Treynor was able to dismiss the risks associated with price and interest rates (Treynor, 1962, p. 4). Treynor realized that the only way that portfolio analysis was able to be conducted was that there was a proxy for the riskless asset (p. 4). In Treynor's consideration of risks affiliated with pricing and rates, those risks were insignificant in the macroeconomy of the United States compared with "typical equity risks" (p. 4).

An important conclusion was that the space where Treynor was experimenting was characterized by only one time period (Treynor, 1962, p. 17). Treynor alluded to multiple time periods concerning residual calculations and considered extrapolation from a single time period to continuous time or multiple time periods; however, the mathematics variables in the proofs started with only a one time period constraint for the proofs (p. 5). These calculations were important to Treynor's theory because these constraints made possible the mathematical result that the lending markets afforded value resolution for the difference between an investor's shares and common equity, since the future value of debt was related to the debt's present value and was a function of the "lending rate" (p. 7).

William Sharpe as a CAPM Primary Theorist

William Sharpe reported that his capital market theory (Sharpe, 1965, p. 417) was not testable in reality because his theory was based upon assets' future expected returns and the risks secondary to the investment of those assets (p. 416). Sharpe realized that the security returns' actual standard deviations and mean values, not expected returns statistics, could be used as a proxy for "*ex ante* predictions of investors" (p. 416). Investor portfolio predictive capability was mentioned elsewhere in Sharpe's work, including a model that could be used for capital asset pricing, inferring that the arguments were linear in scope, and that a prospective investor could achieve a theoretically efficient point anywhere along the "*capital market line*" (Sharpe, 1964, p. 425).

Sharpe had concluded that there was a strong enough correlation coefficient of

0.836, relating annual standard deviation of the funds examined to the average annual fund returns, to show that there was substantiation for one of the standard assumptions of portfolio theory regarding investor risk aversion (Sharpe, 1965, p. 417). If diversification were rational investor behavior to mediate risk assumption, then there were two price choices in the open market: the rate of interest of price timing and the rate of return associated, per unit of risk pricing, known as the "price of risk" (Sharpe, 1964, p. 425).

John Lintner as a CAPM Primary Theorist

Lintner noted that portfolio theory included the ideas that risky assets would trade in a market that was: competitive; under perfect conditions; and that security prices existed in a general equilibrium (Lintner, 1965b, p. 587). Each risky asset's price was linearly related to the security's future expected returns, as well as to the covariances and variances when considering the other securities in the examined securities portfolio (p. 587). The security's value was related to the return wherein each security's total risk was the additive value of the dollar return variance divided by the periodicity of holding added to the "combined covariance of its return with that of all other securities" (p. 587). Lintner accepted the Sharpe observation of the dual price points available in the actual market, but differed from Sharpe's view of capital asset pricing in that these observations would be consistent in general equilibrium even when investors did not share the typically expected identical expectations of future returns (p. 587).

Lintner also observed that assets not held in cash were not related to risk-averse investors' holding of cash in a Gaussian or normal distribution of returns in

competitive markets; however, this was not always necessarily so (Lintner, 1965a, p. 13).

Lintner's view seemed to possess ambivalent duality because Lintner confirmed the idea

that normality should be assumed for the single time period, experimental space because

the basic platform's functionality assumed an asset base that was risk-free and

consequently that "probability judgments are normally distributed" (Lintner, 1965b, p.

588).

Jan Mossin as a CAPM Primary Theorist

Jan Mossin assumed a general equilibrium model for the model for capital asset

pricing (Mossin, 1966, p. 769). Mossin concurred with earlier interpretations of the

model and the associated theory concerning observations by theorists such as Sharpe,

who had made two basic assumptions similar to Treynor's observations: that there was

in-place a proxy for the risk-free interest rate used by all investors and that future

expectations of security returns expected by all investors were identical (p. 770). Mossin

supported the Markowitz assumptions that investors had a range of choices that could be

shown as points on a graph of the securities' "mean-variance" (p. 770) and that expected

returns and yield variances were to be depicted in some basic unit of measure to which he

ascribed the use of the U.S. dollar for convenience (p. 770); this basic measure of the use

of the U.S. dollar was used in this study.

General CAPM Observations

The CAPM was useful for part of this study's methodology because the CAPM risk *beta* calculation results have been found to be useful in evaluating a variety

of return intervals of data from months to years of data examined (Shelor & Wright,

2011, p. 4). One of the issues concerning the use of the CAPM was found to be that the

use of the model involved actual returns data but that the platform for the use of the

CAPM predicated the use of expected returns; investors were found to expect a positive

return from a security since it would be irrational for an investor to invest in risky assets

where the expected return on the risky asset would only be equivalent to the risk-free rate

(Morelli, 2012, p. 48). This observation was an important reason why the CAPM was a

part of the methodology, but that there were other methodological tools used in this

study. The CAPM was only one part of the methodology used in this study because the

CAPM did not test the *ex post* relationship between risk and return (p. 49).

Stephen Ross as an APT Primary Theorist

Stephen Ross developed an alternative to the CAPM, which was introduced

concurrently by Treynor, Lintner, Mossin, and Sharpe, and Ross' arbitrage model had

been in development by Ross as early as 1971 (Ross, 1976, p. 341). Ross realized that the

CAPM was then currently accepted as a method for examining assets that were risky in

"capital markets" (p. 341). Ross altered the name of his alternative theory, for pricing

capital market risky assets, to arbitrage pricing theory (APT) and also recognized that the

CAPM had been derived concurrently and independently by Treynor, Lintner, Sharpe,

and Mossin (Roll & Ross, 1980, p. 1073). Ross noted that his APT was empirically

testable whereas the CAPM was not (p. 1073).

Ross concluded that most of the risk assumed by investors, when investors were inclined to diversify their investment portfolios, was attributable to macroeconomic, "systematic influences" (Chen, Roll, & Ross, 1986, p. 383). Ross used asset substitutes in the application of his APT model and he determined that, given equal pricing of substitutes in the portfolio that were perfect, the principal feature of the APT was that a security's return was identified by restrictions "generated by the model" (Roll & Ross, 1980, p. 1077). Ross reasoned that those restricted model security returns were influenced by various macroeconomic surprises or what he described to be the systemic influences above. The influences were changes to "industrial production" (known as U.S. GNP) (Chen, Roll, & Ross, 1986, p. 386), "inflation" (p. 388), an artificially constructed variable that was the result of subtracting the long-term return of a government bond portfolio's return from the long-term return of bonds that were considered "low-grade" (a proxy for changes in consumer confidence, relative to equity stocks) (p. 389), "term structure" (p. 389), short term "relative pricing" (of various equities) (p. 390), and yield curve changes in "consumption [and] oil prices" (p. 390). Macroeconomic variables *per se* were not used in this study, so Ross' APT model was not applicable to or used in this study.

Carhart Four-Factor Model

In the measure of whether the use of the three-factor Fama and French model or the Carhart four-factor model, which included an extra or fourth factor of momentum, was better at evaluating and predicting the *alpha* and *beta* of securities under examination, it was found that the three-factor model was a better tool for use

in such prediction and evaluation (Elton, Gruber, & Blake, 2011, p. 366). The Carhart

model was not used in this study because the Carhart model's fourth factor, known as

momentum, allowed the researcher to adjust the three-factor model such that the Carhart

four-factor model was found to be better at explaining the returns on mutual funds as

opposed to the results involving individual securities; individual securities, not mutual

funds, were under examination in this study (Pan, 2011, p. 201).

Fama-French Three-Factor Model

The use of the three-factor Fama and French model demonstrated that the

involved risk *beta* was found to be related in a positive way with a firm's projected

growth (a moderate correlation among those variables involved) so that multicollinearity

regarding those book and market variables used, the same as what was used in this study,

did not present difficulties when used with "multivariate regression models" (Mukherji &

Youngho, 2013, p. 50). It was found that when factors, such as those that were used in

this study (for example, risk *beta* from the three-factor model and the size of the firm or

market capitalization), were regressed, that there was a significant, positive correlation

(Kim & Qi, 2010, p. 938). The above consideration was important when the data were

collected and analyzed during this study. There was found to be no association between

the historical quality of return accruals for a security and the future market return of a

security when the three-factor model was used as an examination tool (p. 938). This

consideration was not a concern because the data, when collected and analyzed, proved to be normally distributed with the use of only a very few data plugs.

Studies conducted using publicly traded U.S. utility securities' data from before the 2006-2008 economic upheaval timeframe were characterized by faulty cost of capital estimates when post-regression CAPM model residuals were examined; the rationale given was that when the ordinary least squares (OLS) method was used, it was inappropriate for use with non-normal data characterized by "skewness and kurtosis" (Mcdonald, Michelfelder, & Theodossiou, 2010, p. 375). Normality was not an issue for publicly traded U.S. electric utility company securities data from the years 2010, 2011, and 2012 once the data was collected, analyzed, and a very few data plugs were used.

Gaps in Research and Electric Utility Companies

Relationships have already been established between market value-to-book value (MVBV) and the return-on-equity (ROE) variables (Prado-Lorenzo, Rodriguez-Dominguez, Gallego-Alvarez, & Garcia-Sanchez, 2009, p. 1143), but no investigator has combined MVBV and ROA in publicly traded U.S. electric utility companies. The gap that was closed in the literature was the finding of a relationship between MVBV and ROA for publicly traded U.S. electric utility companies so that a treatment with a study-based Excel computer model process could be used to change a company's debt-ratio to promote investor initial investment. The stated gap that was closed in the literature by using this study revealed relationship between market value, book value and the ROA for publicly traded U.S. electric utility companies was necessary so that a study-based Excel computer model process could then be used to reduce debt-ratios to promote investor initial investment. The promotion of investor initial investment was important because firms compete for growth funds, since investors have alternative investment choices (Mondher, 2011, p. 194), and company debt-ratios do affect investor investment choices (p. 194).

There were found to be different varieties of the over 3,273 electric utility companies in the United States (McNerney, 2007, para. 2) and publicly traded U.S. electric utility companies were chosen as the study's population for several reasons. U.S. consumers rely upon electrically generated power and such "investor-owned utilities...help [to] maintain the infrastructure for the public sector" (McGowan, 2011, para. 1). "Investor-owned utilities are vital to the infrastructure of the country" (McGowan, 2011, para. 3). These observations were important because publicly traded U.S. electric utility companies were found to comprise 6% of all U.S. electric companies, had 38% of the total generating capacity, and served 71% of the U.S. public (McNerney, 2007, para. 15).

Furthermore, of the 210 of such companies, the ones that provided access to their data (reporting to the Securities and Exchange Commission (SEC)) were the publicly-traded variety (160 of the 210, the others were privately held so that there was no access to those financials) (McNerney, 2007, paras. 15-16). From an effect-size and power determination using G-Power 3.0.10 (a statistics software program-please see Appendix C), using a correlation, point biserial model, a representative sample for a t-test correlation study to then later extrapolate to the population by one order of magnitude was a 16 company sample from the population of those 160 publicly reporting companies. The selection was within the parameters necessary to achieve an input power of 0.95 and a large effect size of 0.7071068 with an actual power for the study of 0.960221.

Summary

The intent of the study was to determine a means of realistic, relative (Damodaran, 2006, p. 15), firm valuation and securities repricing for all investors. The repricing was accomplished by examining the relationship between any combination of firm valuation variables using market value, book value, and return on assets (ROA) (Chou et al., 2009, p. 193). The examination enabled the finding of high market-to-book value (Shim et al., 1994, p. 150), publicly traded U.S. electric utility companies in a manner different from traditional techniques for such electric company valuation (Wang, 2008, p. 546). The finding of high market-to-book value companies through this study allowed a study-based Excel computer model process to be used to determine the amount of synthetic assets necessary (Gubler, 2011, p. 68), with the use of derivatives (Gubler, 2011, p. 97), to reorient those companies' debt-ratios since the amount of company debt has been shown to directly bear upon short-term performance and returns (Ozel, 2010, p. i). This short-term business revaluation intercession may eventually be the impetus necessary to eliminate investor satiation and to promote an investors' resurgence of capital direct investment in those companies (Rondinelli & Burpitt, 2000, p. 181).

Once investor capital movement has reoriented the company to a low market-to-book value company, then the common sense need for the synthetic assets

would have been eliminated and the derivative positions could be closed. The theory

above has larger societal applications for the evaluation of all securities (inferential) in

the marketplace with regard to firm revaluation, repricing of the associated securities, and

prospective inclusion of those securities in a private investor or institutional investment

portfolio. This study's results and conclusions hold the potential to positively and

constructively affect social change. Millions of investors have the opportunity to use the

study's tools to mitigate or minimize losses concerning publicly traded securities and the

accompanying securities' returns might more closely mirror the investors' expected

returns.

   The preceding literature review of the salient topics that addressed parts of this

study were: historical research in the Field of Financial Economics and modern portfolio

theory; historical research on relative pricing and valuation; prior research; this study's

control variables; theories, financial models, and propositions related to this study; and

issues such as electric utility companies. The mechanics of the methodology of this study

were addressed more closely in the following Chapter Three methodology section.

Chapter 3: Research Method

Introduction

Statement of the Problem

Investors invested an initial investment in publicly-traded common stock and expected the eventual recovery of the initial investment, which was not the case when the companies underlying the purchased securities were delisted from securities exchanges (Armstrong et al., 2011, p. 52). Investors lost their initial investment, and the profits associated with investment securities, even though investors expected an initial investment to be repaid along with an investment profit for an expected return (Haymore, 2011, p. 1312). A refinement of the specific problem was the analysis of publicly traded U.S. electric utility companies' data because such utilities were integral to the U.S. economy (McGowan, 2011, para. 3).

Prudent investors would not overpay for an initial investment in a company's security, but hypothetical models were shown to overvalue prospective investor payments for public and private resource securities that were model calculated to be overpriced (Morrison & Brown, 2009, p. 307). The Stage 1 security relative pricing allowed the finding of priced publicly-traded U.S. electric utility companies that provided electricity resources. The company securities were intended to be model study repriced in Stage 2 to reflect the actual debt accrued but not completely reported by the underlying company (Arends, 2010, para 1, 6) to give investors better value for their initial investment.

Relationships have already been established between MVBV and the ROE variables (Prado-Lorenzo et al., 2009, p. 1143), but no investigator has combined MVBV and ROA in publicly-traded U.S. electric utility companies. The gap I closed in the literature was the finding of a relationship between MVBV and ROA for publicly-traded U.S. electric utility companies for treatment with a study-based Excel computer model process to change a company's debt-ratio to promote investor initial investment.

Purpose of the Study

The purpose of this quantitative study was to determine the company pricing and securities investment suitability of a randomly selected sample of 16 publicly traded U.S. electric utility companies. The study design included correlations and multiple regression analyses to support the three-factor, Fama-French, multiple regression model (Muiño & Trombetta, 2009, p. 88). No survey instrument was used because the data were randomly collected from the geographic population of the 160 publicly traded U.S. electric utility companies in the Electronic Data Gathering, Analysis, and Retrieval (EDGAR) database. Data reliability was supported by federal law compliance in the reporting of each firm's annual 10-K. A validity threat might have been the value-weighting of security portfolios in the Fama-French regression equation (You & Zhang, 2009, p. 574), but portfolio security holding compensated for that concern and cross-sectional data analysis negated unnatural portfolio variance returns (You & Zhang, 2009, p. 575).

Research Questions and Hypotheses

The earning of an economic profit meant that a publicly-traded U.S. electric utility company made profits above and beyond the company's basic cost of capital, known as EVA, which eventually resulted in higher future company profitability (Abdel-Jalil & Thuniebat, 2009, p. 26). The stated earnings would have been (per year) more than the static required return on invested capital.

There were five sets of hypotheses. The first set dealt with an underpriced situation compared with ROA. The second set dealt with overpriced results compared with ROA. The third set dealt with whether a publicly-traded U.S. electric utility company, with a debt-ratio higher than the ideal range upper limit of 60% (Eiteman et al., 2007, p. 434), was the same as an overpriced, publicly-traded U.S. electric utility company. The fourth set dealt with whether or not a derivative induced, synthetically created asset moved a publicly-traded U.S. electric utility company from an overpriced to an underpriced status. The fifth set dealt with whether there was a relationship between a publicly-traded U.S. electric utility company's nontraditional, relative pricing, a study derived computer model's variant pricing of the company, and the company's market capitalization (please see Appendix A).

1. What was the relationship between low market-to-book value (threshold - the market-to-book ratio is a ratio less than 1:1) publicly-traded U.S. electric utility companies and their 3-year annualized average return on assets?

$H_0 1$: There is no relationship between low market-to-book value (threshold - the market-to-book ratio is a ratio less than 1:1) publicly-traded U.S. electric utility companies and their 3-year annualized average return on assets.

$H_1$1: There is a relationship between low market-to-book value (threshold - the market-to-book ratio is a ratio less than 1:1) publicly-traded U.S. electric utility companies and their 3-year annualized average return on assets.

The research design for the first set of hypotheses was to demonstrate, with a two-tailed, t-test correlation and multivariate and bivariate regression studies, that there was a relationship between the independent variables of market value and book value to the dependent variable of ROA.

2.   To what extent was there a relationship between high market-to-book value (threshold - the market-to-book ratio is a ratio of 1:1 or more) publicly-traded U.S. electric utility companies and their 3-year annualized average return on assets?

$H_0$2: There is no relationship between high market-to-book value (threshold - the market-to-book ratio is a ratio of 1:1 or more) publicly-traded U.S. electric utility companies and their 3-year annualized average return on assets.

$H_1$2: There is a relationship between high market-to-book value (threshold - the market-to-book ratio is a ratio of 1:1 or more) publicly-traded U.S. electric utility companies and their 3-year annualized average return on assets.

The assembled moderating variable of MVBV and the annual ROA variable, for the 3 years of 2010, 2011, and 2012 for each of the sample's relevant 16 publicly-traded U.S. electric utility companies, was intended to be analyzed with the use of the Pearson's *r* correlation analysis to operationalize the constructs of the first and the second sets of hypotheses.

3.　To what extent was there a relationship between a publicly-traded U.S. electric utility company, which was leveraged above a 60% debt-ratio, and a high market-to-book value (threshold - the market-to-book ratio is a ratio of 1:1 or more) publicly-traded U.S. electric utility company?

$H_0$3: There is no relationship between a publicly-traded U.S. electric utility company leveraged above 60% and a high market-to-book value publicly-traded U.S. electric utility company.

$H_1$3:There is a relationship between a publicly-traded U.S. electric utility company leveraged above 60% and a high market-to-book value publicly-traded U.S. electric utility company.

To operationalize the constructs of the third set of hypotheses, with regard to the 16 company sample, the list of companies leveraged above 60% was compared to the list of high market-to-book value companies. Data plugs were used to normalize the data (please see the data handling section of this paper). The means of comparison for the 3 years of 2010, 2011, and 2012, for the relevant sample's 16 publicly-traded U.S. electric utility companies, was an intended study with the use of the Pearson's *r* correlation analysis to operationalize the constructs of the third set of hypotheses.

4.　To what extent was the use of derivatives necessary to move a publicly-traded U.S. electric utility company from a high market-to-book value to a low market-to-book value status?

$H_0$4: There is no relationship between the use of a derivative induced, synthetic asset treatment to move a publicly-traded U.S. electric utility company from a high market-to-book value to a low market-to-book value.

$H_1$4: There is a relationship between the use of a derivative induced, synthetic asset treatment to move a publicly-traded U.S. electric utility company from a high market-to-book value to a low market-to-book value.

The operationalization of the constructs regarding the fourth set of hypotheses was accomplished differently from the operationalization of the previous three sets of hypotheses constructs. The reason for the different approach with the fourth set of hypotheses was that a synthetic asset was created to change the debt-ratio of the firms leveraged above 60% in the 16 company sample of publicly-traded U.S. electric utility companies. A version of the three-factor, Fama-French, multiple regression model was used to operationalize the fourth set of hypotheses constructs (Fama & French, 2004, p. 38). Control variables used in operationalizing the previous three sets of hypotheses with covariance analyses were not necessary to operationalize the fourth set of hypotheses constructs because the use of the Fama-French regression equation took into account the necessary market and firm specific factors by default (Fama & French, 2004, p. 38).

5.   To what extent was there a relationship between a publicly-traded U.S. electric utility company's nontraditional, relative pricing, a study derived computer model's variant pricing of the company, and the company's

market capitalization (see Appendix A)?

$H_0$5: There is no relationship between a publicly-traded U.S. electric utility company's non-traditional, relative pricing, a study derived computer model's variant pricing of the company, and the company's market capitalization.

$H_1$5: There is a relationship between a publicly-traded U.S. electric utility company's non-traditional, relative pricing, a study derived computer model's variant pricing of the company, and the company's market capitalization.

The fifth set of hypotheses dealt with whether there was a relationship between a publicly-traded U.S. electric utility company's nontraditional, relative pricing, a study derived computer model's variant pricing of the company, and the company's market capitalization (please see Appendix A). The variables to be regressed were the results of the CAPM estimate of a company's security price, for each of the 16 sample companies, the associated variant price that included the accounting for the actual debt accrued by the sample company, and that company's market capitalization figure.

Research Methods and Design

A fundamental concept in the Field of Economics has been the difference between the considerations of the short-term and the long-term, but there has been no fixed time period assigned to each of these terms by economists (Samuelson & Nordhaus, 1995, p. 98). The short-term was a period where alterable production input factors could be changed, but not the "fixed factors" (Samuelson & Nordhaus, 1995, p. 98). The long-term was a period where all input factors, including capital, could be changed (Samuelson &

Nordhaus, 1995, p. 98). A useful practitioner economic short-term period, for

capital considerations, was found to be 3 years (Campbell & Selden, 2000, p. 2). Three

distinct time points were necessary to perform a trend determination and 3 years of data

were collected from each of the 16 companies in the sample in order to examine trending

in this study (Guillot & Fung, 2010, p. 569).

Preparatory calculations gave investigators insight into datasets and reduced

potential errors in the study when the collected data were analyzed (Aczel &

Sounderpandian, 2009, p. 289). An F test multivariate regression (Aczel &

Sounderpandian, 2009, pp. 473-474), using the Statistics Package for the Social Sciences

(SPSS) software package (GradPack version 17.0), hereinafter referred to as the *software*,

was intended to be performed on the data collected from the 16 publicly-traded U.S.

electric utility companies to confirm a relationship between the dependent ROA variable

and either the book value or the market value independent variables (Aczel &

Sounderpandian, 2009, p. 475). Except for certain cases where a high coefficient of

determination (R^2) was incorrect (Aczel & Sounderpandian, 2009, p. 441), the ANOVA

table resulting from the performed regression showed a high coefficient of determination

to reveal the regression results' suitability and certainty concerning a further examination

of the data collected (Aczel & Sounderpandian, 2009, p. 440). The significance level of

the study was 0.05 meaning that there was a 95% confidence level that the null

hypothesis would be false (Aczel & Sounderpandian, 2009, p. 263). When the p-value in

the ANOVA table output was less than the 0.05 significance level value, then the null hypothesis, that the means of all three data variables were equal, was rejected

because a linear relationship was revealed between the independent variable of ROA and

at least one of the dependent variables of book value and market value (Aczel &

Sounderpandian, 2009, p. 474).

The regression results' suitability and confidence prompted the use of descriptive

statistics to obtain more insight into the data collected by reviewing the data groups to

recognize tendencies, make meaningful connections, and detect anomalies (Aczel &

Sounderpandian, 2009, p. 29). The software was used to generate a box plot to determine

each data group's "central tendency, spread, skewness, and the existence of outliers"

(Aczel & Sounderpandian, 2009, p. 31). The software allowed further analysis of the data

for dispersion, kurtosis, and other statistics (Aczel & Sounderpandian, 2009, p. 36). The

data variables of book value, market value, and ROA, revealed by the regression and

descriptive statistics analyses findings, were either positively correlated if the ROAs were

above the industry sector goal or negatively correlated if the ROAs were below the

industry sector goal (Chou et al., 2009, p. 194).

Given the finding of a positive or negative relationship above, since the proxy for

the p-value was less than .05 and not equal to zero (rejecting a null hypothesis), a

confirmation of results was applied with a two-tailed t-test distribution and a more

succinct relationship examination of the data collected was with the intended use of a

Pearson's r correlation analysis (Aczel & Sounderpandian, 2009, pp. 430-432).

Operationalization of the constructs tested in a basic way each of the first three hypotheses of this study.

A moderating variable was assembled, from the variables of market value and book value (MVBV) (Creswell, 2009, p. 50). MVBV has been useful as a proxy in other studies for the non-traditional, relative valuation of firms (Prado-Lorenzo, Rodriguez-Dominguez, Gallego-Alvarez, & Garcia-Sanchez, 2009, p. 1134; Gentry & Shen, 2010, p. 514) and the accompanying repricing of securities. MVBV has also been useful as a proxy in firm under- or overvaluation (Shim et al., 1994, p. 150). Investigators have commonly used accounting measures, such as ROA, in the evaluation of corporate performance and those measures have helped to determine corporate valuation; the use of such accounting measures was determined to be still valid (Alkhalialeh, 2008, p. 246).

The assembled moderating variable of MVBV and the annual ROA variable, for the three years of 2010, 2011, and 2012 for each of the sample's relevant 16 publicly traded U.S. electric utility companies, was analyzed to operationalize the constructs of the first, second, and third sets of hypotheses. Until the data were collected, there was no means of determining how many of the firms in the 16 company sample of publicly traded U.S. electric utility companies was by definition low market-to-book value, high market-to-book value or mispriced. According to the definitions, the low market-to-book value (threshold - the market-to-book ratio is a ratio less than 1:1) companies were to be used to address the first set of hypotheses and the high market-to-book value (threshold - the market-to-book ratio is a ratio of 1:1 or more) companies were be used to address the second set of hypotheses. Since the statistical analyses of the operationalized constructs for hypotheses one and two would involved a means test (Newton & Rudestam, 1999, p. 73) and would involve some correlation studies, an effect size larger than .30 was anticipated (Newton & Rudestam, 1999, p. 75).

An overleveraged company for the study was a firm that had a debt-ratio percentage above 60% (Eiteman, Stonehill, & Moffett, 2007, p. 434). A high market-to-book value company was a firm that had a MVBV equal to or greater than a ratio of 1:1 (Shim et al., 1994, p. 150). Many well managed publicly traded United States firms have a reported debt-ratio of between 30 and 60 percent (Eiteman et al., 2007, p. 434) and U.S. firms reported that they each have an average cumulative debt-ratio of 50 percent (Arends, 2010, para. 10). However, when financial analysts have read the parenthetical notes on firm balance sheets and had then accounted for the actual debt reported off-balance sheet by these same reporting firms, the actual calculated debt-ratio became 80 percent (Arends, 2010, paras. 1 and 6). A debt-ratio calculation was performed on the data from each of the annual 10-K sets of financial statements, for the sample's 16 publicly traded U.S. electric utility companies, reported to the Electronic Data Gathering, Analysis, and Retrieval (EDGAR) database provided by the Securities and Exchange Commission (SEC) online. The study methodology was not originally intended to rely upon the company reported, debt-ratio percentage for each company for the years 2010, 2011, and 2012.

The previous analyses performed on the first, second, and third sets of hypotheses generated a considerable amount of findings. This quantitative study addressed spurious variables (Creswell, 2009, p. 51) and included control variables (p. 51) with a covariance analysis (p. 51) in order to triangulate the study's findings (Lee, Ng, & Swaminathan, 2009, p. 316). A triangulation of the analyses of the operationalized constructs of the first three sets of hypotheses reduced the ambiguity of results (Lee, Ng, & Swaminathan, 2009, p. 316). A multivariate analysis of covariance (MANCOVA) was performed on the variables already analyzed in each of the first three sets of hypotheses constructs (Berkman & Reise, 2012, pp. 205-206). For each of the operationalized constructs of the first three sets of hypotheses, control variables were added to the MANCOVA (p. 207).

The operationalization of the construct regarding the fourth set of hypotheses was accomplished differently from the operationalization of the previous three sets of hypotheses constructs. The reason for the different approach with the fourth set of hypotheses was that a synthetic asset was created to change the debt-ratio of the firms with a debt-ratio percentage above 60% in the 16 company sample of publicly traded U.S. electric utility companies. A version of the three-factor, Fama-French, multiple regression model was used to operationalize the fourth set of hypotheses constructs (Fama & French, 2004, p. 38). Control variables used in operationalizing the previous three sets of hypotheses with covariance analyses were not necessary to operationalize the fourth set of hypotheses constructs since the use of the Fama-French regression equation took into account the necessary market and firm specific factors by default (p. 38).

The fifth set of hypotheses dealt with whether there was a relationship between a publicly traded U.S. electric utility company's non-traditional, relative pricing, a study derived computer model's variant pricing of the company, and the company's market capitalization (please see Appendix A). The originally intended capstone of the study was the intended writing of a computer optimization model in Excel that would use the j factor as a predictor to optimize a firm's releveraging and non-traditional, relative revaluation with synthetic assets. In this way, a j-index would then be created for the general marketplace so that for a one percent move in debt-ratio leverage adjustment, such that when the capital units were known, the amount of capital needed for the firm, in millions or billions of U.S. dollars, would be a concrete, actual figure for use in the Field of Finance.

Data Collection

Since the data collected was public domain, single stage sampling was used to collect the data and a random sample was recommended because "with randomization, a representative sample from a population provides the ability to generalize to a population" (Creswell, 2009, p. 148). The data involved only one stratum since all of the data collected came from the same type of the previously discussed, publicly traded U.S. electric utility companies. Instead of tables to assure the random selection of companies for data collection, a computerized random number generator was employed. The means of performing this function was the serialization of the entire population of the 160 publicly traded U.S. electric utility companies (please see Appendix B) in an Excel spreadsheet and the use of an Excel random number generator that assured the randomness of the selection of the 16 company sample.

One of the assumptions of this study was to utilize a reverse order of magnitude (a reduction of the population by one order of magnitude, or a factor of ten), so that inferential statistics were then used for generalization of the results in Chapter Four of the DM to relate the sample's results to the population sampled. A company sample size of 16 publicly traded U.S. electric utility companies for comparison to a population of 160 publicly traded U.S. electric utility companies was an ideal sample size. A means of verifying the correlation's accuracy was the Durbin-Watson test for "first-order error autocorrelation" (Aczel & Sounderpandian, 2009, p. 540), wherein the given statistical alpha's level examined for that α was 0.05. The observed correlation was large enough so that the p1 value was smaller than the alpha 0.05 threshold noted above so that the *p*-value was $p1 < 0$ or $p1 > 0$ (two critical points). The autocorrelation, in the case of a resulting positive correlation, reinforced the previously discussed magnitude assumption for the study's generalization of results from the sample to the population.

No survey instrument, pre-existing or created, was used since the data were publicly available and were inanimate financial figures. The variables, however, require further discussion. An assumption in this study was that corporate profits were important to the firm's management and to shareholders according to the philosophy contained within the shareholder wealth maximization (SWM) model, which included the notion that "the firm should strive to maximize the return to shareholders" (Eiteman, Stonehill,

& Moffett, 2007, p. 4). Market value and book value were important to corporate valuation issues since a market value that was lower than the firm's book value was assumed to indicate an undervalued or mispriced security that might be appropriate for inclusion in an investment portfolio to earn greater profits for shareholders (Shim et al., 1994, p. 150; Bodie, Kane, & Marcus, 2005, p. 291).

The author of Johnstone (2007) noted that the use of the capital asset pricing model (CAPM) was not always appropriate since that use addressed only certain cases of valuation, due to unadjusted currency, because the units of currency varied significantly between *ex ante* and *ex post* valuation (p. 159). A similar observation was noted elsewhere in the literature concerning the use of traditional valuation techniques (Grauer, 2008, p. 150), and in certain circumstances regarding equity valuation, the "price to book value is the best standalone price multiple" (Sehgal & Pandey, 2010, p. 68). To expand upon current finance theory, regarding the valuation of financial instruments from domestic companies, this study was a variation of and expansion upon the three-factor, Fama-French, multiple regression technique already in accepted use (Mirza & Afzal, 2011, p. 173).

The two independent variables of market value and book value were combined into one moderating variable (Creswell, 2009, p. 50) so that it was appropriate to use a *t*-test to look for relationships between the serialized groups of data: one independent variable, which was constructed for this study, and one dependent variable (p. 153).

Materials/Instruments

The purpose of this quantitative study was to determine the company pricing and securities investment suitability of a randomly selected sample of 16 publicly traded U.S. electric utility companies. The study design included correlations and multiple regression analyses to support the three-factor, Fama-French, multiple regression model (Muiño & Trombetta, 2009, p. 88). No survey instrument was used because the data was randomly collected from the geographic population of the 160 publicly traded U.S. electric utility companies in the Electronic Data Gathering, Analysis, and Retrieval (EDGAR) database. Data reliability was supported by federal law compliance in the reporting of each firm's annual 10-K. A validity threat could have been the value-weighting of security portfolios in the Fama-French regression equation (You & Zhang, 2009, p. 574), but portfolio security holding compensated for that concern and the cross-sectional data analysis negated unnatural portfolio variance returns (You & Zhang, 2009, p. 575).

The appropriateness of the research method was that it expanded upon current finance theory, regarding the valuation of financial instruments from domestic companies, and this study was a variation of and expansion upon the three-factor, Fama-French, multiple regression technique already in accepted use (Mirza & Afzal, 2011, p. 173). A survey of the literature indicated that much of this research has been previously performed, but that specific research has not been performed with a study-based Excel computer model process on publicly traded U.S. electric utility company securities (Prado-Lorenzo, Rodriguez-Dominguez, Gallego-Alvarez, & Garcia-Sanchez, 2009, p.

1133). Furthermore, the research has been performed with MVBV and ROE, but not with MVBV and ROA (Afza, Slahudin, & Nazir, 2008, p. 7; Clubb & Naffi, 2007, p. 1; Gentry & Shen, 2010, p. 514).

No survey instrument, pre-existing or created, was used since the data were publicly available and were inanimate financial figures. The variables, however, require further discussion. An assumption for this study was that corporate profits were important to the firm's management and to shareholders according to the philosophy contained within the shareholder wealth maximization (SWM) model, which included the notion that "the firm should strive to maximize the return to shareholders" (Eiteman, Stonehill, & Moffett, 2007, p. 4). Market value and book value were important to corporate pricing issues since a market price that was lower than the firm's book price was assumed to indicate an underpriced security that might be appropriate for inclusion in an investment portfolio to earn greater profits for shareholders (Shim et al., 1994, p. 150; Bodie, Kane, & Marcus, 2005, p. 291).

The various types of measures to assess financial performance of the firm and the firm's accompanying financial instruments have been discussed, explained, and verified (Gentry & Shen, 2010, p. 520). Correlation coefficients were used in the first stage of the study, to establish a positive or negative relationship between the various measures, and some second stage analysis was used as a verification, or confirmation step, to aid in the establishment of a causal relationship by using several forms of regression studies (p. 522). There has been a continuing debate among scholars concerning the relationship between the measures of firm performance and the resulting performance of the associated securities of those firms examined; a medium positive correlation for a variety of industries within an industry has been confirmed (p. 522). The findings mentioned were relevant to this study because the methodology used by the investigators in Gentry and Shen (2010), which was a two-pronged approach of a correlation study and a confirming set of regression studies, was the same and provided the methodological and theoretical platform for this study. Similar to this study, the Gentry and Shen (2010) findings provided a platform for the study of relationships between an accounting measure of firm profitability, such as book value, and a market measure of firm profitability, such as market value, along with the creation of a moderating variable, such as MVBV. Furthermore, the investigators in Gentry and Shen (2010) compared those analyzed variables' findings with the short term accounting measure of profitability known as ROA; similar to this study.

Operational Definition of Variables

There were two independent variables, which were more commonly known as market value and book value. The fair market value data variable was the per share amount evaluation by the public marketplace of what the equity was worth concerning a publicly traded company (Stickney & Weil, 2003, p. 899). The book value, in this case the book value per share of common stock (diluted–please see Appendix A), was the compilation of asset valuation by *accounting standards* so that the resulting amount determined by subtracting liabilities from assets, or the resulting equity, was then divided by the number of shares outstanding to arrive at the figure for the second independent variable (p. 875). The dependent variable was the return-on-assets (ROA) variable. ROA was particularly useful in portfolio theory because the ROA was the "net income plus after-tax interest charges plus minority interest income divided by average total assets; perhaps the single most useful ratio for assessing management's overall operating performance" (p. 935). The two independent variables of market value and book value were combined into one moderating variable (Creswell, 2009, p. 50) so that it was appropriate to use a two-tailed t-test to look for relationships between the serialized groups of data: one independent variable, which was constructed for this study, and one dependent variable (p. 153).

The first variable, which was an independent variable, was the earnings assessment, or market price, of the company's market value. The second variable, also an independent variable, was a non-earnings accounting assessment because it was the book value, or price per share (diluted), of the security. When these two variables were coupled into a ratio, the result amounted to a number less than, equal to, or greater than one. The reason for coupling these two variables was to develop an easily seen relationship between the notional, or book price of the security, and the perceived value placed upon the security by the marketplace's perception of that security. The third variable was the dependent variable because the answers to the two previous variables determined the answer to this third variable (MVBV).

Market Price 1. The fair market price data variable was the per share amount evaluation by the public marketplace of what the equity was worth concerning

a publicly traded company (Stickney & Weil, 2003, p. 899). The variable was from the

ratio scale since the numbers were financial data from the New York Stock Exchange

(NYSE) ending share prices for the corporate security in question (typically December

31st). The range was in U.S. dollars from zero to hundreds of dollars.

Book Value 2. The book price data variable, in this case the book value per share

of common stock, was the compilation of asset valuation by accounting standards so that

the resulting amount determined by subtracting liabilities from assets, or the resulting

equity, was then divided by the number of shares outstanding to arrive at the figure for

the second independent variable (Stickney & Weil, 2003, p. 875). The variable was from

the ratio scale since the numbers were financial data from the Electronic Data Gathering,

Analysis, and Retrieval (EDGAR) database provided by the Securities and Exchange

Commission (SEC) online derived from company financial reports. The range was in

U.S. dollars from zero to hundreds of dollars.

Return-on-Assets (ROA) 3. The dependent variable was the return-on-assets

(ROA) variable. ROA was particularly useful in portfolio theory because the ROA was

the "net income plus after-tax interest charges plus minority interest income divided by

average total assets; perhaps the single most useful ratio for assessing management's

overall operating performance" (Stickney & Weil, 2003, p. 935). The two independent

variables of market price and book price were combined into one moderating variable

(Creswell, 2009, p. 50) so that it was appropriate to use a *t*-test to look for relationships

between the serialized groups of data: one independent variable, which was
constructed for this study, and one dependent variable (p. 153). The range was in U.S.
dollars from zero to hundreds of dollars divided by U.S. dollars from zero to hundreds of
dollars resulting in a percentage figure.

Non-Traditional, Relative Firm Price (NTRFP) 4. The moderating variable of
MVBV became the non-traditional, relative firm price variable for each of the publicly
traded U.S. electric utility companies in the 16 company sample. The NTRFV variable
was a ratio numerical variable in that each of the 16 companies in the sample was
determined to be, as a result of the study's analysis, either over- or underpriced.

Computer Model Variant of Company Pricing (CMVCP) 5. The study-created
computer optimization model, written with the use of Excel, used the Fama-French
regression equation variant to devise a *j*-index. The *j*-index was mathematically a residual
rectifier that in effect balanced the Fama-French regression equation's results and the
residual rectifier *j*-index was a ratio-scale real number (a single or double digit that was
either positive or negative). The *j*-index was depicted mathematically as a percentage
and, to be of value, generally required simultaneous presentation with an explanatory
mathematical set theory equivalent for each company to establish a basis for computation
efficiency and effectiveness and to convey an accurate meaning for the computational
result.

Company Market Capitalization (CMC) 6. Although market capitalization has
been generally considered by financial analysts in the common marketplace to be a ratio-

scale variable in dollars, to make the MANCOVA a workable statistical

analysis in this study, the ratio-scale data required conversion. The ratio-scale market

capitalization for each company in the 16 company sample of publicly traded U.S.

electric utility companies was converted to a categorical variable in the following manner

(please see Appendix A). If a sample firm's market capitalization was found to be equal

to or less than one billion dollars (U.S.), then the firm was listed as a small capitalization

company (Small Cap) and the data point was represented by a "1." If the market

capitalization of a sample firm was found to be greater than one billion dollars (U.S.), but

less than 5 billion dollars (U.S.), then the firm was listed as a medium capitalization

company (Medium Cap) and the data point was represented by a "2." If the market

capitalization of a sample firm was found to be equal to, or greater than 5 billion dollars

(U.S.), then the firm was listed as a large capitalization company (Large Cap) and the

data point was represented by a "3."

Data Analysis

An *F* test multivariate regression (Aczel & Sounderpandian, 2009, pp. 473-474),

using the Statistics Package for the Social Sciences (SPSS) software package (GradPack

version 17.0), hereinafter referred to as the *software*, was intended to be performed on

some of the data collected from the 16 publicly traded U.S. electric utility companies to

confirm a relationship between the dependent ROA variable and either the book value or

the market value independent variables (Aczel & Sounderpandian, 2009, p. 475). Since

the *p*-value in the ANOVA table output was less than the 0.05 significance level value, then the null hypothesis, that the means of all three data variables are equal, was rejected because a linear relationship was revealed between the independent variable of ROA and at least one of the dependent variables of book value and market value (Aczel & Sounderpandian, 2009, p. 474).

The software was used to generate a box plot to determine each data group's "central tendency, spread, skewness, and the existence of outliers" (Aczel & Sounderpandian, 2009, p. 31). The software allowed further analysis of the data for dispersion, kurtosis, and other statistics (Aczel & Sounderpandian, 2009, p. 36).

Given the finding of a positive or negative relationship above, since the proxy for the p-value was less than .05 and not equal to zero (rejecting a null hypothesis), a confirmation of results was applied with a two-tailed t-test distribution and a more succinct relationship examination of the data collected was intended with the use of a Pearson's r correlation analysis (Aczel & Sounderpandian, 2009, pp. 430-432). Operationalization of the constructs tested in a basic way each of the first three sets of hypotheses constructs of this study.

A moderating variable was assembled, from the variables of market value and book value (MVBV) (Creswell, 2009, p. 50). MVBV has also been useful as a proxy in firm under- or overvaluation (Shim et al., 1994, p. 150). Investigators have commonly used accounting measures, such as ROA, in the evaluation of corporate performance and those measures have helped to determine corporate valuation; the use of such accounting measures was determined to be still valid (Alkhalialeh, 2008, p. 246).

The assembled moderating variable of MVBV and the annual ROA variable, for the three years of 2010, 2011, and 2012 for each of the sample's relevant 16 publicly traded U.S. electric utility companies, was intended to be analyzed with the use of the Pearson's r correlation analysis to operationalize the constructs of the first and the second sets of hypotheses. Until the data were collected, there was no means of determining how many of the firms in the 16 company prospective sample of publicly traded U.S. electric utility companies would be by definition low market-to-book value, high market-to-book value or mispriced. According to the definitions, the low market-to-book value (threshold - the market-to-book ratio is a ratio less than 1:1) companies would be used to address the first set of hypotheses and the high market-to-book value (threshold - the market-to-book ratio is a ratio of 1:1 or more) companies would be used to address the second set of hypotheses.

A debt-ratio calculation was performed on the data from each of the annual 10-K sets of financial statements, for the sample's 16 publicly traded U.S. electric utility companies, reported to the Electronic Data Gathering, Analysis, and Retrieval (EDGAR) database provided by the Securities and Exchange Commission (SEC) online. The study was not originally intended to rely upon the company reported, debt-ratio percentage for each company for the years 2010, 2011, and 2012.

To operationalize the constructs of the third set of hypotheses, with regard to the 16 company sample, the list of companies leveraged above 60% was compared to the list of high market-to-book value companies. Data plugs were used (please see the data handling section of this paper). The means of comparison for the three years of 2010, 2011, and 2012, for the relevant sample's 16 publicly traded U.S. electric utility companies, was intended to be a study with the use of the Pearson's *r* correlation analysis to operationalize the constructs of the third set of hypotheses.

The previous analyses performed on the first, second, and third sets of hypotheses generated a considerable amount of findings. This quantitative study addressed spurious variables (Creswell, 2009, p. 51) and included control variables (p. 51) with a covariance analysis (p. 51) in order to triangulate the study's findings (Lee, Ng, & Swaminathan, 2009, p. 316). A triangulation of the analyses of the operationalized constructs of the first three sets of hypotheses reduced the ambiguity of the results (Lee, Ng, & Swaminathan, 2009, p. 316). A multivariate analysis of covariance (MANCOVA) using the software was performed on the variables already analyzed in each of the first three sets of hypotheses constructs (Berkman & Reise, 2012, pp. 205-206). For each of the operationalized constructs of the first three sets of hypotheses, control variables were added to the MANCOVA that was used principally on the hypothesis three constructs (p. 207).

The first control variable was the calculated ratio scale continuous variable of company-specific risk (*beta*) derived with the use of the capital asset pricing model (CAPM) depicted in equation 3.1 (Fama & French, 2004, p. 29).

$$E(R_i) = R_f + [E(R_M) - R_f]\,\beta_{iM},\ i = 1, \ldots, N.$$

Equation 3.1

The formula for the calculation of the individual company security *beta* (β_i) was depicted in equation 3.2 (Bodie, Kane, & Marcus, 2005, p. 327).

$$\beta_i = \frac{\text{Cov}\ (R_i,\ R_M)}{\text{Var}\ (R_M)}$$

Equation 3.2

The second control variable was a categorical variable proxy for the ratio scale variable of investor satiation more commonly known as market capitalization (please see Appendix A). The third control variable was a continuous ratio scale variable depicted as a percentage of total asset impairment shown as a percentage remainder from the market value of company-wide total assets for each firm, which was originally assumed to be a reduced, non 100 percent variable (as opposed to the found 100 percent constant) since the 10-K reports were required to legally report all debt. The three control variables were used in the MANCOVA performed on the sample companies' data, for the years 2010, 2011, and 2012, in the 16 company sample of publicly traded U.S. electric utility companies.

Company-specific risk was calculated for the years 2010, 2011, and 2012 for each of the 16 companies in the sample with the use of the CAPM in order to mathematically determine the risk *beta* for each firm using equation 3.2. Based upon efficient market theory, the proxy for investor satiation was each firm's market capitalization and firms were classified into a categorical variable with the categories of small cap, medium cap, and large cap categories (please see Appendix A). The amount of asset impairment for each company, for the years 2010, 2011, and 2012 as a percentage number from the annual 10-K financial statements of the 16 firms in the study sample, was determined to be zero (a 100 percent constant – all debt was accounted for in the financials). Once the MANCOVA analysis was run on the hypotheses constructs and the findings were tabulated and reviewed, the control variables were removed from the covariance analyses of the hypotheses three constructs because of signal-to-noise considerations (Berkman & Reise, 2012, p. 220).

The operationalization of the constructs regarding the fourth set of hypotheses was accomplished differently from the operationalization of the previous three sets of hypotheses constructs. The reason for the different approach with the fourth set of hypotheses was that a friction-less synthetic asset payout was used to change the debt-ratio of the firms leveraged above a 60% debt-ratio in the 16 company sample of publicly traded U.S. electric utility companies back to 50%. A version of the three-factor, Fama-French, multiple regression model was used to operationalize the fourth set of hypotheses constructs by finding the *betas* (Fama & French, 2004, p. 38). Control variables used in operationalizing the previous three sets of hypotheses with covariance analyses were not necessary to operationalize the fourth set of hypotheses constructs since the use of the Fama-French regression equation took into account the necessary market and firm specific factors by default (p. 38).

The Fama-French regression equation involved the use of data plugs (Fama & French, 2004, p. 38). The first data plug on the right side of the equation was the expected market return ($E(R_{Mt})$) variable and the second data plug was the risk-free return (R_{ft}) variable. The ($E(R_{Mt})$) and (R_{ft}) data plugs were available online, as were all of the computed data plugs used below, from the open-access, public data portion of the website provided by Eugene Fama, one of the originators of the Fama-French regression equation used in this study. A third data plug necessary for the right side of the equation was the returns remainder of a portfolio of large stocks subtracted from a portfolio of small stocks (SMB_t); both portfolios were diversified (Fama & French, 2004, p. 38). The fourth data plug necessary for the right side of the equation was the returns remainder of a portfolio of low market-to-book stocks subtracted from a portfolio of high market-to-book stocks (HML_t); both portfolios were diversified (Fama & French, 2004, p. 38). The data plugs of ($E(R_{Mt})$), (R_{ft}), (SMB_t), and (HML_t) were all annually computed data streams, from the year 1927 to the present, available from the Fama and French public domain data site online (http://mba.tuck.dartmouth.edu/pages/faculty/ken.french/).

The remaining variables in the Fama-French equation were not all data plugs and the non data plug variables used were the Consumer Price Index (CPI) figures commonly available (see Appendix D). The first calculated variable for use in the equation was the excess firm security return, for each of the 16 firms in the sample for years 2010, 2011, and 2012, and was calculated as each firm's annual ROA (R_{it}) minus the annualized risk-free rate of return (R_{ft}) data plug. The firms' annual ROAs were calculated from each respective firm's financial statements provided by the SEC's EDGAR database. The second calculated variable for use in the equation was the excess market return and was calculated as the annual market return (R_{Mt}) data plug minus the annualized

risk-free rate of return (R_{ft}) data plug from the French datastream. In order to calculate the

slopes (*betas*) for the Fama-French equation, a multiple regression analysis was

performed by regressing the excess security return ((R_{it}) - (R_{ft})) variable on the variables

of excess market return ((R_{Mt}) - (R_{ft})), small minus big (SMB_t), and high minus low

(HML_t) (Fama & French, 2004, pp. 38-39). Part of the results from the multiple

regression analysis were the *betas* of β_0, β_{iM}, β_{is}, and β_{ih}, variable*s* shown in the complete

Fama-French multiple regression equation, which was described below as equation 3.3

(Fama & French, 2004, p. 38).

$$E(R_{it}) - R_{ft} = \beta_0 + \beta_{iM}[E(R_{Mt}) - R_{ft}] + \beta_{is}E(SMB_t) + \beta_{ih}E(HML_t)$$

Equation 3.3

The results from the calculations and findings of the analyses associated with the

operationalization of the constructs of the first three sets of hypotheses, in the prospective

16 companies of the sample of publicly traded U.S. electric utility companies, were used

to calculate how much capital must be injected into the balance sheet of the companies in

that sample by firm with the use of the synthetic asset derivatives. The reason that the

company samples were injected with synthetic asset capital was to theoretically move the

overleveraged companies back to the moderately leveraged 50 percent debt-ratio

originally reported by U.S. firms (Arends, 2010, para. 10). The financial statements of the

companies under consideration were partially recast for the figures to determine the

adjusted, non-traditional, relative valuation for each company that was injected with synthetic capital. The purpose for the recalculation and the partial recasting of each affected firm's financial statements was to determine if the releveraging of those applicable firms, in the 16 company sample, had each moved from a firm leveraged above 60% to a moderately leveraged status and if those same companies had also moved from an overpriced to an underpriced status. A bivariate regression was performed on those theoretically calculated firm repricings and firm releverings to look for relationships to complete the operationalization of the fourth set of hypotheses.

The notion that U.S. firms had reported a 50 percent debt-ratio, but actually had an 80 percent debt-ratio (Arends, 2010, paras. 1 and 6), logically meant that the mathematical difference between the reported leverage and the calculated debt leverage would lead to an inequality in the Fama-French, multiple regression equation. The finance practitioner response to that basic observation logically meant that the expected return of a firm's security ($E(R_{it})$) from equation 3.5 would not equal that same firm's actual, annual return (ROA). To compensate for the inequality in the practical use of equation 3.3, a rectifier residual term was introduced into the right-hand side of the equation, now depicted as equation 3.4 (Berkman & Reise, 2012, p. 208). The residual term j was a positive or negative real number, somewhere within the range of $\{-\infty \leq 0 \leq \infty\}$, and was hereinafter below referred to as the variable known as j. The Fama-French regression equation, including the residual variable term j, a term which would obviously be a percentage, was re-written as equation 3.4.

$$E(R_{it}) - R_{ft} = \beta_0 + \beta_{iM}[E(R_{Mt}) - R_{ft}] + \beta_{is}E(SMB_t) + \beta_{ih}E(HML_t) + j$$

Equation 3.4

Equation 3.4 re-written for mathematical computation, to simply show the expected security return by itself on the left side as a dependent variable, involved the addition of the risk-free rate plug variable to both sides of the equation. The risk-free rate algebraically canceled on the left, and result in equation 3.4, which was similar to some permutations of the original Fama-French equation but with different goals and terms (Fama & French, 2004, p. 39), was rewritten as equation 3.5.

$$E(R_{it}) = R_{ft} + \beta_0 + \beta_{iM}[E(R_{Mt}) - R_{ft}] + \beta_{is} E(SMB_t) + \beta_{ih} E(HML_t) + j$$

Equation 3.5

The residual term j compensated for the difference between the original equation's change in excess return by providing a factor that depicted the dependent variable more accurately after the releveraging and repricing of each specific firm and the firm's associated equity security by year in the 16 company sample. The two prospective changes to equation 3.3 theoretically balanced the equation, in light of the fundamental changes to each firm's equity security pricing and leverage, in order make the calculation of each firm's expected return synonymous with the actual return.

The capstone of the study was the intended writing of a computer optimization model in Excel that used the theoretical j factor as a predictor to optimize a firm's releveraging and non-traditional, relative revaluation with synthetic assets. In this way, a j-index would have been created for the general marketplace so that for a one percent move in debt-ratio leverage adjustment, when the capital units were known, the amount of capital needed for the firm, in millions or billions of U.S. dollars, would be

a concrete, actual figure for use in the Field of Finance. The j-index, the computer

optimizer model, and equation 3.5 would all be prospectively useful in inferentially

optimizing the debt-ratio, valuation, and capital requirements of publicly traded U.S.

electric utility companies in any portfolio. With the injection of more data and a study

expansion, the indices, models, and equations conceivably had implications for expansion

to the rebalancing and revaluation of all publicly traded companies such that the

prospective price of the firm's associated equity securities would more accurately reflect

the security's market value, as opposed to the actual market price. Thus, the prospective

allusion would obviously be that the firm's securities would be a good purchase for an

investment portfolio. To complete the analysis, the repricing of the sample's securities

was conducted with the CAPM model mathematical calculations.

Methodological Assumptions, Limitations, and Delimitations

Assumptions

One of the assumptions of this study was to utilize a reverse order of magnitude (a

reduction of the population by one order of magnitude, or a factor of ten), so that

inferential statistics were used for generalization of the results in Chapter Four of the

dissertation manuscript (DM) to relate the sample's results to the population sampled

(Creswell, 2009, p. 148). A company sample size of 16 publicly traded U.S. electric

utility companies for comparison to a population of 160 publicly traded U.S. electric

utility companies was appropriate. A means of verifying the correlation's accuracy was the Durbin-Watson test for "first-order error autocorrelation" (Aczel &

Sounderpandian, 2009, p. 540), wherein the given statistical *alpha's* level examined for

that α was 0.05. The observed correlation was large enough so that the p1 value was

smaller than the *alpha* 0.05 threshold noted above so that the *p*-value was p1 < 0 or p1 >

0 (two critical points). The autocorrelation, in the case of a resulting positive correlation,

reinforced the previously discussed magnitude assumption for the study's generalization

of results from the sample to the population.

No survey instrument, pre-existing or created, was used since the data were

publicly available and were inanimate financial figures. The variables, however, required

further discussion. An assumption in this study was that corporate profits were important

to the firm's management and to shareholders according to the philosophy within the

shareholder wealth maximization (SWM) model, which contained the notion that "the

firm should strive to maximize the return to shareholders" (Eiteman, Stonehill, &

Moffett, 2007, p. 4). Market value and book value were important to corporate pricing

issues since a market price that was lower than the firm's book price was assumed to

indicate an underpriced security that might be appropriate for inclusion in an investment

portfolio to earn greater profits for shareholders (Shim et al., 1994, p. 150).

The author of Johnstone (2007) noted that the use of the capital asset CAPM was

not always appropriate since that use addressed only certain cases of pricing, due to

unadjusted currency, because the units of currency varied significantly between *ex ante*

and *ex post* valuation (p. 159). A similar observation was noted elsewhere in the literature concerning the use of traditional pricing techniques (Grauer, 2008, p. 150),

and in certain circumstances regarding equity pricing, the "price to book value is the best

standalone price multiple" (Sehgal & Pandey, 2010, p. 68). To expand upon current

finance theory, regarding the pricing of financial instruments from domestic companies,

this study was a variation of and expansion upon the three-factor, Fama-French, multiple

regression technique already in accepted use (Mirza & Afzal, 2011, p. 173).

The two independent variables of market value and book value were combined

into one moderating variable (Creswell, 2009, p. 50) so that it was appropriate to use a

two-tailed t-test to look for relationships between the serialized groups of data: one

independent variable, which was constructed for this study, and one dependent variable

(p. 153).

Limitations

There were two independent variables, which were more commonly known as

market value and book value. The fair market value data variable was the per share

amount evaluation by the public marketplace of what the equity was worth concerning a

publicly traded company (Stickney & Weil, 2003, p. 899). The book value, in this case

the book value per share of common stock (diluted–please see Appendix A), was the

compilation of asset valuation by *accounting standards* so that the resulting amount

determined by subtracting liabilities from assets, or the resulting equity, was then divided

by the number of shares outstanding to arrive at the figure for the second independent

variable (p. 875). The dependent variable was the return-on-assets (ROA) variable. ROA was particularly useful in portfolio theory because the ROA was the "net income plus after-tax interest charges plus minority interest income divided by average total assets; perhaps the single most useful ratio for assessing management's overall operating performance" (p. 935). The two independent variables of market value and book value were combined into one moderating variable (Creswell, 2009, p. 50) so that it was appropriate to use a two-tailed t-test to look for relationships between the serialized groups of data: one independent variable, which was constructed for this study, and one dependent variable (p. 153).

The first variable, which was an independent variable, was the earnings assessment, or market price, of the company's market value. The second variable, also an independent variable, was a non-earnings accounting assessment because it was the book value, or price per share (diluted), of the security. When these two variables were coupled into a ratio, the result amounted to a number less than, equal to, or greater than one. The reason for coupling these two variables was to develop an easily seen relationship between the notional, or book price of the security, and the perceived value placed upon the security by the marketplace's perception of that security. The third variable was the dependent variable because the answers to the two previous variables determined the answer to this third variable (MVBV).

Market Price 1. The fair market price data variable was the per share amount evaluation by the public marketplace of what the equity was worth concerning a publicly traded company (Stickney & Weil, 2003, p. 899). The variable was from the ratio scale since the numbers were financial data from the New York Stock Exchange

(NYSE) ending share prices for the corporate security in question (typically December

31st). The range was in U.S. dollars from zero to hundreds of dollars.

Book Value 2. The book price data variable, in this case the book value per share

of common stock, was the compilation of asset valuation by accounting standards so that

the resulting amount determined by subtracting liabilities from assets, or the resulting

equity, was then divided by the number of shares outstanding to arrive at the figure for

the second independent variable (Stickney & Weil, 2003, p. 875). The variable was from

the ratio scale since the numbers were financial data from the Electronic Data Gathering,

Analysis, and Retrieval (EDGAR) database provided by the Securities and Exchange

Commission (SEC) online derived from company financial reports. The range was in

U.S. dollars from zero to hundreds of dollars.

Return-on-Assets (ROA) 3. The dependent variable was the return-on-assets

(ROA) variable. ROA was particularly useful in portfolio theory because the ROA was

the "net income plus after-tax interest charges plus minority interest income divided by

average total assets; perhaps the single most useful ratio for assessing management's

overall operating performance" (Stickney & Weil, 2003, p. 935). The two independent

variables of market price and book price were combined into one moderating variable

(Creswell, 2009, p. 50) so that it was appropriate to use a *t*-test to look for relationships

between the serialized groups of data: one independent variable, which was constructed

for this study, and one dependent variable (p. 153). The range was in U.S. dollars from zero to hundreds of dollars divided by U.S. dollars from zero to hundreds of

dollars resulting in a percentage figure.

Non-Traditional, Relative Firm Price (NTRFP) 4. The moderating variable of

MVBV became the non-traditional, relative firm price variable for each of the publicly

traded U.S. electric utility companies in the 16 company sample. The NTRFV variable

was a ratio numerical variable in that each of the 16 companies in the sample was

determined to be, as a result of the study's analysis, either over- or underpriced.

Computer Model Variant of Company Pricing (CMVCP) 5. The study-created

computer optimization model, written with the use of Excel, used the Fama-French

regression equation variant to devise a *j*-index. The *j*-index was mathematically a residual

rectifier that in effect balanced the Fama-French regression equation's results and the

residual rectifier *j*-index was a ratio-scale real number (a single or double digit that was

either positive or negative). The *j*-index was depicted mathematically as a percentage

and, to be of value, generally required simultaneous presentation with an explanatory

mathematical set theory equivalent for each company to establish a basis for computation

efficiency and effectiveness and to convey an accurate meaning for the computational

result.

Company Market Capitalization (CMC) 6. Although market capitalization has

been generally considered by financial analysts in the common marketplace to be a ratio-

scale variable in dollars, to make the MANCOVA a workable statistical analysis in this

study, the ratio-scale data required conversion. The ratio-scale market capitalization for each company in the 16 company sample of publicly traded U.S. electric

utility companies was converted to a categorical variable in the following manner (please

see Appendix A). If a sample firm's market capitalization was found to be equal to or less

than one billion dollars (U.S.), then the firm was listed as a small capitalization company

(Small Cap) and the data point was represented by a "1." If the market capitalization of a

sample firm was found to be greater than one billion dollars (U.S.), but less than 5 billion

dollars (U.S.), then the firm was listed as a medium capitalization company (Medium

Cap) and the data point was represented by a "2." If the market capitalization of a sample

firm was found to be equal to, or greater than 5 billion dollars (U.S.), then the firm was

listed as a large capitalization company (Large Cap) and the data point was represented

by a "3."

Delimitations

Since the data collected was from the public domain, single stage sampling was

used to collect the data and a random sample was recommended because "with

randomization, a representative sample from a population provides the ability to

generalize to a population" (Creswell, 2009, p. 148). The data involved only one stratum

since all of the data collected was from the same type of the previously discussed,

publicly traded U.S. electric utility companies. Instead of tables to assure random

selection of companies for data collection, a computerized random number generator was

employed. A means of performing this function was the serialization of the entire

population of the 160 publicly traded U.S. electric utility companies in an Excel spreadsheet and the use of an Excel random number generator to assure the randomness of the selection of the 16 company sample. The use of the computer program Excel was not the only part of the study's analyses, but those calculations were found in similar studies to be an important part of those studies (Shelor & Wright, 2011, p. 6). The size of this study's sample, only 16 companies, was found to be an insufficient amount of data to support a study involving investor withdrawals – it was assumed that there would be no withdrawals of the capital invested in sample securities for this study (Pfau, 2012, p. 36).

The purpose of this quantitative study was to analyze a sample of 16 publicly traded U.S. electric utility companies and to extrapolate the study's results, via generalization, to the population of 160 publicly traded U.S. electric utility companies (Creswell, 2009, p. 148). A survey instrument was not used because the data was collected from the public domain. The purpose for the collection of data from the public domain was that this data was the same audited data provided to potential investors, making it available to anyone who may become an eventual end-user; individual investors, financial intermediaries, and portfolio managers. The data collection was cross-sectional in that the data was collected all at once. The collection method was "structured record reviews to collect financial…information" (Creswell, 2009, p. 146).

A financial records review for the years 2010, 2011, and 2012 was performed because the costs of collection was negligible or non-existent, the data was public domain and available to anyone for potential analysis, and it was convenient for any potential researcher to confirm and verify the results from the dissertation manuscript

(DM). Researchers in the Field of Finance have long accepted the notion that quantitative

studies, as opposed to qualitative or mixed-method studies, were performed on ratio-

scale, financial data because "in the quantitative analysis we can bring the predictions of

the theory closer to the observed properties of the data" (Olivero, 2010, p. 403). The use

of the research design in this study was a variant of the three-factor, Fama-French,

multiple regression technique already in accepted use (Mirza & Afzal, 2011, p. 173). The

reason that annual data for three years was collected in this study was that the risk *beta*

for the CAPM part of the study concerned equity securities, representative of the electric

utility companies in the sample of this study, and the period for the collection of that

annual data was shown to be three years of data when examining price changes of

individual securities (Shelor & Wright, 2011, p. 4).

There were different varieties of the over 3,273 electric utility companies in the

United States (McNerney, 2007, para. 2) and publicly traded U.S. electric utility

companies were chosen as the study's population for several reasons. U.S. consumers

were found to rely upon electrically generated power and such "investor-owned

utilities…help [to] maintain the infrastructure for the public sector" (McGowan, 2011,

para. 1). "Investor-owned utilities are vital to the infrastructure of the country"

(McGowan, 2011, para. 3). These observations were important because publicly traded

U.S. electric utility companies were found to comprise 6% of all U.S. electric companies,

had 38% of the total generating capacity, and served 71% of the U.S. public (McNerney,

2007, para. 15).

Furthermore, of the 210 of such companies, the ones that provided access to their data (reporting to the Securities and Exchange Commission (SEC)) were of the publicly-traded variety (160 of the 210, the others were privately held so that there was no access to those financials) (McNerney, 2007, paras. 15-16). From an effect-size and power determination using G-Power 3.0.10 (a statistics software program-please see Appendix C), using a correlation, point biserial model, a representative sample for a *t*-test correlation study to then later extrapolate to the population by one order of magnitude (Creswell, 2009, p. 148) was a 16 company sample from the population of those 160 publicly reporting companies. The selection was within the parameters necessary to achieve an input power of 0.95 and a large effect size of 0.7071068 with an actual power for the study of 0.960221.

Ethical Assurances

The author of Mondher (2011) noted that Merton Miller and Franco Modigliani sparked the birth of modern financial theory with the introduction of the theorem of capital structure in 1958, which was the foundation for the CAPM and most contemporary finance theory (p. 193). However, current literature authors have disagreed with the use of *ex-ante* and *ex-post* capital valuation in studies where the traditional CAPM was combined with the Fama-French Model (Muiño & Trombetta, 2009, p. 88). There have been scholarly disagreements regarding the use of traditional financial models, in conjunction with the use of the accounting variables of return-on-equity

(ROE) and return-on-assets (ROA), and previously accepted traditional firm valuation techniques (Rachdi & Ameur, 2011, p. 88). The author of Johnstone (2007) noted that the use of the CAPM was not always appropriate, since that use only addressed certain cases of valuation, due to unadjusted currency, because the units of currency varied significantly between *ex ante* and *ex post* valuation (p. 159).

The above observations from the literature prompted a plan for the dissertation manuscript (DM) that compensated for those observed shortcomings by the use of the following. Econometric data calibration (Angrist & Pischke, 2009, p. 114) was planned to be used to solve the *ex ante* and *ex post* valuation issue (Johnstone, 2007, p. 159). Book value and market value firm variables were used, which have greater explanatory power for firm investment security returns than the use of the CAPM (Clubb & Naffi, 2007, p. 1), along with relative, corporate, security valuation (Damodaran, 2006, p. 15), for all investors and stakeholders. A prospective relationship was sought between firm valuation, using those market value and book value variables, and the firm's return-on-assets (ROA) as a variable (Chou et al., 2009, p. 193). A form of relative, non-traditional, firm valuation (Damodaran, 2006, p. 3) and repricing was used, in conjunction with the three-factor, Fama-French, multiple regression technique already in accepted use (Mirza & Afzal, 2011, p. 173), to solve the scholarly disagreement issue concerning the use of accounting, market, and traditional firm variables, and the related security, valuation techniques (Rachdi & Ameur, 2011, p. 88) and pricing techniques. The uses in the DM, delineated above, moved finance theory, and finance application, closer toward achieving a more reliable and true firm security valuation (Damodaran, 2007, p. 3) and price.

The general rule for the generalization of the start date of a theory, such as in the literature review of the DM, which was applied to the start date and publication referenced for the literature review's beginning, was the agreed upon date and literature piece promulgated by mutual scholarly agreement in the literature itself (Duran, Eisenhart, Erickson, Grant, Green, Hedges, Levine, Moss, Pellegrino, & Schneider, 2006, p. 39). To hold to the acceptable standard of care, integrity, and ethical standards for the literature review in the DM, authors in the literature have noted that the acceptable standard was to employ the use of large databases and key words in the topic field to perform searches on the topic to be analyzed so that a thorough literature review could be accomplished (Horner & Minifie, 2011, p. 307).

The review of the literature focused upon the scholarly writings from the introduction in 1952 by Markowitz of modern portfolio theory (MPT) to the present. However, finance theory was formally introduced, by economists Merton Miller and Franco Modigliani, with the introduction of the theorem of capital structure in 1958 (Mondher, 2011, p. 193). The authors of Samuelson and Nordhaus (1995) discussed the same theoretical corollary when they noted that classical economics mandated that, with certain assumptions, as the accepted propensity to invest increased the capital stock, the capital's efficiency declined to the current rate of interest (p. 251). Several assumptions, regarding firm security valuation and pricing similar to the views of the authors just mentioned, were made in the DM.

Research Guidelines for Care, Integrity and Ethical Standards

Human subjects or animals were not used in the DM, but there was the use of inanimate financial data from the public domain. Those financial data were collected from the Electronic Data Gathering, Analysis, and Retrieval (EDGAR) database provided by the Securities and Exchange Commission (SEC). The sample firms were to be notified upon completion of the DM, concerning the firm data analyzed in the DM, even though the securities data were listed in the public domain, to make certain that the companies involved were aware of the use of such data. The general research and publication guidelines, for the DM rules, were specific concerning care, integrity and ethical standards (American Psychological Association, 2011, paras. 1, 2, 6, & 7). Standard Eight, of the publication guidelines, did mandate a debriefing (American Psychological Association, 2011, Standard 8.08, sections a-c). Even though the data used in the DM was inanimate, public domain data, the research went beyond the Standard Eight requirement just noted, and a completed DM was to be provided to each of the companies from which data was used for analysis in the DM. The additional step meant, for the DM, that companies would have a copy of the completed publication, in which their data had been used, as a sign of good faith from academia.

The general research and publication guidelines, for the writing of the DM rules, were specific concerning care, integrity and ethical standards (Committee on Science, Engineering, and Public Policy (U.S.), National Academy of Sciences (U.S.), National

Academy of Engineering., & Institute of Medicine (U.S.), 2009, p. ix). The

institute's guidelines were even more specific about the writing guidelines for a study,

such as the DM, with the provision of a comprehensive list that constituted a number of

steps to be followed in the writing of such studies and research for publication

(Committee on Science, Engineering, and Public Policy (U.S.), National Academy of

Sciences (U.S.), National Academy of Engineering., & Institute of Medicine (U.S.),

2009, p. 32). The DM research went beyond the steps just mentioned, in the writing of

the DM, with the use of a three-pronged writing strategy. The first prong of that strategy

was to write a particular chapter of the DM. The second prong was to summarize that

DM text with a piece of computer software, commonly known as the Copernic

Summarizer, which summarized the text's key points. The third prong was to further

summarize that text printout with a prose rewrite of the summarized text. The three-prong

approach just depicted helped to: prevent plagiarism; eliminate rambling prose; focus on

the key points of each paragraph; and shorten the DM considerably.

Summary

The general problem was that investors invested an initial investment in publicly

traded common stock and expected the eventual recovery of the initial investment, which

was not the case when the companies underlying the purchased securities were delisted

from securities exchanges (Armstrong et al., 2011, p. 52). The specific problem was that

investors lost their initial investment, and the associated investment securities profits,

even though investors expected an initial investment to be repaid along with an investment profit for an expected return (Haymore, 2011, p. 1312). The specific problem analysis involved publicly traded U.S. electric utility companies' data because such utilities were integral to the U.S. economy (McGowan, 2011, para. 3).

Prudent investors would not overpay for an initial investment in a company's security, but hypothetical models in studies were shown to overvalue prospective investor payments for publicly traded securities that were model calculated to be overpriced (Morrison & Brown, 2009, p. 307). The stage one security relative pricing revealed priced publicly traded U.S. electric utility companies that provided electricity resources. The company securities were computer model study repriced in some stage two analyses to reflect the actual debt accrued but not completely reported by the underlying company (Arends, 2010, paras. 1 and 6) to give investors better value for their initial investment. This study's results and conclusions hold the potential to positively and constructively affect social change. Millions of investors have the opportunity to use the study's tools to mitigate or minimize losses concerning publicly traded securities and the accompanying securities' returns might more closely mirror the investors' expected returns.

Relationships have already been established between market value-to-book value (MVBV) and the return-on-equity (ROE) variables (Prado-Lorenzo, Rodriguez-Dominguez, Gallego-Alvarez, & Garcia-Sanchez, 2009, p. 1143), but no investigator has combined MVBV and ROA in publicly traded U.S. electric utility companies. The gap that was closed in the literature was the finding of a relationship between MVBV and ROA for publicly traded U.S. electric utility companies for treatment with a study-based

Excel computer model process to change a company's debt-ratio to promote

investor initial investment. These and other considerations were addressed in the ensuing

Chapter Four results section of this study.

Chapter 4: Results

The financial turmoil of 2006-2008 led U.S. firms to report debt-ratios that differed from the debt-ratios accrued. Investors bought common stock expecting initial investment return and lost money when companies delisted. The specific problem was the further loss of investment securities profits. There was a lack of research to aid investors with debt-ratios in the relative pricing of publicly-traded U.S. electric utility company securities. The purpose of this research was to determine the pricing of a sample of securities with the application of synthetic assets and company debt accrued. The research questions concerned whether company securities (a) were underpriced compared with ROA, (b) were overpriced compared with ROA, (c) with a debt-ratio higher than 60% were also overpriced, (d) with a synthetic asset added became underpriced, and (e) with relative pricing related to variant pricing and market capitalization. The study's theoretical framework was based upon Pan's EMH of price change prediction concerning the differences between real market security prices and multifactor model price predictions. In this quantitative study, the accounting and financial data of 16 EDGAR database publicly-traded U.S. electric utility companies was used to determine securities pricing and the investment suitability using correlations, multiple regression analyses, the addition of synthetic assets, and accrued debt. Walden University administration approved the conduct of the research in this DM. The Institutional Review Board (IRB) issued their formal approval number of # 06-12-13-0071095.

In Chapter 4, I present the analytical results of the five research questions' hypothetical constructs and the findings of the analyses of the associated

sample statistics, descriptive statistics, and the results of the individual analyses of each

of those five research questions' sets of hypothetical constructs.

Sample Statistics

The study sample was collected from the 160 firms in the population of firms

serialized in Appendix B. To randomly select a sample of 16 firms, an Excel spreadsheet

randomness command was executed upon the serialized list of firms, serially numbered

from 1 to 160 from Appendix B, and the command was executed 16 times with no

duplicate results (the Excel command used was =RANDBETWEEN(1,160)). To ensure

the level of firm anonymity and protection discussed in Chapter 3, each of the 16 firms of

the sample drawn was then researched in the SEC database of online financial statements

and annual reports, also known as the EDGAR database, wherein each of the 16 firms'

Central Index Keys (CIK) was collected and keyed to the respective firms in the sample.

Once the annual reports for each of the 16 firms for the years of 2010, 2011, 2012 were

collected, the names of the 16 firms and their associated ticker symbols were deleted

from the database (keying the firms to the CIK) and the CIK for each firm was then

truncated from 10 digits down to the last four digits of the CIK sequence to then

anonymously identify each of the 16 firms for data usage and analysis. The final sample

of the 16 firms' annual reports (10-K's) for the years of 2010, 2011, and 2012 for each

firm were then analyzed to obtain the data that were extracted and key-punch entered into

an Excel spreadsheet for analysis in this study. Those data are in the various appendices.

Descriptive Statistics

The first three variables of Market Price (MP1), Book Value price per share (BV2), and Return-on-Assets (ROA3) for the 16 sample firms for the years 2010, 2011, and 2012 were tabulated in SPSS to set a baseline for the raw data collected concerning the central tendency measures of mean, median, and mode. With the baseline results in place, the next step in the descriptive statistics analysis was to test for data outliers in the raw data assembled from the financial statements, concerning the variables of MP1, BK2, and ROA3. Those data were also used to assemble the data for the other three variables used in this study, which were market-to-book price (NTRFP4), variant price (CMVCP5), and market capitalization (CMC6), regarding variables for the 16 sample firms from the years of 2010, 2011, and 2012. The frequency and boxplot results were used in conjunction with the data results' skewness, kurtosis, minima, maxima, and associated range to determine the statistical outliers. The Markowitz process delineated in the Chapter 2, concerning the fact that variance analysis allowed the eradication of the extreme outliers, was used to substitute the variables' means as data plugs for the normalization of those data. The data plug usage was supported by Chapter 3 processes and confirmed by normality tests. The Cronbach alpha analytical results of all six variables' data were used to triangulate the results of the descriptive analyses and to support the reliability and, thereby, the suitability of the use of those normal data in this study.

No econometric recalculation was performed on the 3 years of data for the 16 sample set firms for the years of 2010, 2011, 2012. The rationale for no

econometric calibration was that there were only 3 years of data, the sample set was small

at $n < 30$ (Kanji, 2006, p. 26), and because the CPI (used as a proxy) average change for

the year 2010 was 1.6%, 2011 was 3.2%, and 2012 was 2.1%, obviating the necessity for

econometrics (see Appendix D). Table 1 includes the measures of central tendency and

follows.

Table 1

Mean, Median, Mode (H0: 1-3 Data set Results for the Sample of 16 Firms

	Mean	Median	Mode
MP1_2010	$36.53	$36.31	$19.39
MP1_2011	$41.69	$39.75	$21.78
MP1_2012	$43.71	$42.89	$20.31
MP1_Avg.	$40.65	$39.65	20.49
BV_2010	$26.26	$25.37	$16.59
BV_2011	$27.12	$25.70	$16.78
BV_2012	$30.11	$27.52	$18.01
BV_Avg.	$27.83	$28.47	17.52
ROA3_2010	3.52%	2.75%	0.59%
ROA3_2011	3.53%	2.86%	3.36%
ROA3_2012	2.80%	2.77%	2.97%
ROA3_Avg.	3.28%	2.79%	-0.56%

The results in Table 1 were tabulated in SPSS to set a baseline for the raw data collected from the SEC online database, known as EDGAR, for the data fields in the Excel spreadsheet columns tabulated from the financial statements for the first three variables of MP, BV, and ROA for the 16 sample firms for the years 2010, 2011, and 2012. With the baseline results in place, the next step in the descriptive statistics analysis was to test for data outliers in the raw data assembled from the financial statements, concerning the variables of MP, BK and ROA, for the 16 sample firms from the years of 2010, 2011, and 2012.

Table 2

Frequency/Boxplot Results (H0: 1-3 Data set Results Evaluating for use of Data Plugs)

	Skewness	Kurtosis	Minimum	Maximum	Range	Outliers
MP1_2010	0.292	-1.018	$19.39	$53.43	$34.04	0
MP1_2011	0.481	-0.378	$21.78	$66.00	$44.22	0
MP1_2012	0.496	-0.393	$20.31	$70.94	$50.63	0
MP1_Avg.	0.374	-0.739	$20.49	$61.08	$40.59	0
BV_2010	0.129	-1.391	$16.59	$37.91	$21.32	0
BV_2011	0.246	-1.165	$16.78	$39.18	$22.40	0
BV_2012	1.374	2.459	$18.01	$57.59	$39.58	1
BV_Avg.	0.134	-0.951	$17.52	$38.82	$21.30	0
ROA3_2010	2.946	9.920	0.59%	13.26%	12.67%	3
ROA3_2011	3.118	11.434	-0.08%	14.93%	15.01%	2
ROA3_2012	1.531	7.125	-4.46%	13.76%	18.22%	3
ROA3_Avg.	2.880	10.334	-0.56%	13.98%	14.54%	3

The results in Table 2 were tabulated in SPSS to determine the dataset's skewness, kurtosis, range, and the number of data outliers. Of the various means of dealing with data that exhibited right-skewness (Skewness = MP1_Avg. - 0.374; BV_Avg. - 0.134; ROA3_Avg. - 2.880) and a variability in extreme from slightly platykurtic (Kurtosis = MP1_Avg. - -0.739: BV_Avg. - -0.951) to markedly leptokurtic (Kurtosis = ROA3_Avg. - 10.334), the least invasive (as opposed to taking the square or cube root of all of the data, or of raising all of the data points to some power to obtain normal data distributions) and the least destructive method of cleaning those data was the use of data plugs. This technique dove-tailed with the Markowitz process to eradicate the extreme outliers.

There existed a succinct relationship between the central measure of mean and the data spread standard deviation (Aczel, 2009, p. 24). The data points were calculated from the annual report static figures to prepare the cumulative, aggregated data points for analysis (for example, book value share price was tabulated as: Firm Book Value Price (Variable BK2) = [Total Assets – (Intangible Assets + Total Liabilities)]/Number of common shares outstanding). In light of Chebyshev's Theorem and The Empirical Rule (Aczel, 2009, p. 24), the mean for each SPSS tabulated column of 16 data points for each variable was used as a data plug in the updated analysis sample. The 12 outliers were two to three standard deviations outside of each variable range's minima and maxima for each column of data and the calculated means for the few affected columns were used accordingly as data plugs (one-dozen data plugs in total). The standard deviation was updated for each column in light of the data plugs used and then the average, or mean, of each of the variable's three columns' results were tabulated for each average variable and were used to arrive at each variable's average result for the cumulative variable average (MP1_Avg., BK2_Avg., and ROA3_Avg.). The hundreds of remaining data points were affected insofar as the Central Index Key (CIK) 6160 BV2_2012 data point plug was reflected in an update of the NTRFP4_2012 data point (a constructed data point that used

BV2_2012) and the related NTRFP4_AVG. data point for Central Index Key

(CIK) 6160. The data plugs were mostly in the ROA data (92% of the plugs that were

used) and ROA was not used to construct the remaining study variables in the manner

that the Market Price and Book Price per share were used. The updated results appear in

Table 3 below along with the concomitant tabulated data normality results (updated data

are in Appendices E – J).

Table 3

Frequency/Boxplot Results (H0: 1-3 Data set Results using the Mean Data Plugs)

	Minimum	Maximum	Range	Outliers	$q=w/s$	Normal
MP1_2010	$19.39	$53.43	$34.04	0	$3.16	Yes
MP1_2011	$21.78	$66.00	$44.22	0	$3.59	Yes
MP1_2012	$20.31	$70.94	$50.63	0	$3.41	Yes
MP1_Avg.	$20.49	$61.08	$40.59	0	$3.39	Yes
BV_2010	$16.59	$37.91	$21.32	0	$2.95	No
BV_2011	$16.78	$39.18	$22.40	0	$3.05	Yes
BV_2012	$18.01	$40.88	$22.87	0	$3.28	Yes
BV_Avg.	$17.52	$38.82	$21.30	0	$3.09	Yes
ROA3_2010	1.85%	4.38%	2.53%	0	3.77%	Yes
ROA3_2011	1.20%	4.83%	3.63%	0	4.00%	Yes
ROA3_2012	1.55%	4.06%	2.51%	0	3.92%	Yes
ROA3_Avg.	0.76%	4.21%	3.45%	0	3.90%	Yes

The results in Table 3 were tabulated to determine the dataset's overall normality based upon a conventional mathematical determination of dataset normality known as the w/s-test for normality (Kanji, 2006, p. 74). The statistical test resultant q was the mathematical result of the data column range known as w (maximum – the minimum columnar data point for a particular variable) divided by the standard deviation of the column of data known as s. The resultant q value became the critical value test statistic that was compared to the critical values for such q resultant figures (see Table 3 – the $q = w/s$ column) and Appendix K. Since the level of significance for this study was an alpha of $\alpha \leq 0.05$, when the mathematical q fell between the Appendix K tabular minimum and maximum (in this case, minimum $a = 3.01$ and maximum $b = 4.24$), the data then fell within the parameters of normality and those data were considered to be a normal distribution. Since the variable averages (MP1_Avg., BK2_Avg., and ROA3_Avg.) all fell within the normality parameters of the minimum and maximum for this study's *alpha*, the data for analysis were assumed for this study to be normally distributed in order to allow the use of analytic tests that were applicable to normal data distributions.

To round out the descriptive statistical analytics performed on the data, a coefficient *alpha* (derivation of the Cronbach's *alpha*) analysis was performed on the data, which was a mathematical reliability measure performed upon single sampling events, to determine the reliability of each column of annual data for each year's variable (Yockey, 2011, p. 49). It would have been illogical to perform such an analysis upon the average of those columnar years of data for each variable since the essence of the analytic was designed to compare each of the individual years of a particular variable in order to determine reliability based upon the separate data fields that were then averaged within the test, obviating the need to perform the analytical test upon the averaged data fields (p. 50). The resultant Cronbach figures have been depicted in Table 4 below.

Table 4

Cronbach Alpha Analytical Results (H0: 1-6 Data set Results using Updated Data)

	Mean	Std. Dev.	N	C. Alpha	Adequacy
MP1_2010	$36.53	$10.76	16	0.980	Excellent
MP1_2011	$41.69	$12.33	16	0.980	Excellent
MP1_2012	$43.72	$14.84	16	0.980	Excellent
BV_2010	$26.26	$ 7.23	16	0.964	Excellent
BV_2011	$27.12	$ 7.34	16	0.964	Excellent
BV_2012	$28.39	$ 6.97	16	0.964	Excellent
ROA3_2010	2.93%	0.67%	16	0.845	Good
ROA3_2011	3.04%	0.91%	16	0.845	Good
ROA3_2012	2.77%	0.64%	16	0.845	Good
NTRFP4_2010	1.45	0.54	16	0.915	Excellent
NTRFP4_2011	1.61	0.67	16	0.915	Excellent
NTRFP4_2012	1.53	0.32	16	0.915	Excellent
CMVCP5_2010	-15.12%	4.12%	16	0.771	Fair
CMVCP5_2011	-0.41%	0.13%	16	0.771	Fair
CMVCP5_2012	-14.12%	3.86%	16	0.771	Fair
CMC6_2010	$10.478B	$17.261B	16	0.962	Excellent
CMC6_2011	$12.531B	$21.388B	16	0.962	Excellent
CMC6_2012	$10.370B	$12.241B	16	0.962	Excellent

The results in Table 4 were tabulated to determine the dataset's reliability with regard to item and scale and two-thirds of the analytical results were found to be excellent indicating that there was a very high reliability, as measured by the analysis of the coefficient *alpha,* in the collection and processing of the data points for analysis in this study.

Results of the Tests of Hypotheses

Hypothesis 1

$H_0 1$: There is no relationship between low market-to-book value (threshold - the market-to-book ratio is a ratio less than 1:1) publicly-traded U.S. electric utility companies and their 3-year annualized average return on assets.

$H_1 1$: There is a relationship between low market-to-book value (threshold - the market-to-book ratio is a ratio less than 1:1) publicly-traded U.S. electric utility companies and their 3-year annualized average return on assets.

Stage 1 of the Study

Preliminary results of *t*-test paired samples statistics of MP1_AVG and BV2_AVG data were that the three-year securities average market price ($M = 40.65$, $SD = 12.51$) was significantly more important than the three-year securities average book price ($M = 27.83$, $SD = 6.78$), $t(15) = 5.93$, p < .05, $d = 1.48$. The paired sample correlation result was 0.753, p < .05. The results of this analysis indicated a resultant tested *p*-value that was significant at less than .05, so the null hypothesis was rejected.

Preliminary results of *t*-test paired samples statistics of MP1_AVG and

ROA3_AVG data were that the three-year securities average market price (M = 40.65, SD = 12.51) was significantly more important than the three-year securities average Return-on-Assets (ROA) (M = 2.75, SD = 0.80), $t(15)$ = 12.15, p < .05, d = 3.04. The paired sample correlation result was 0.077, p = 0.776. The results of this analysis indicated a resultant tested p-value that was significant at less than .05, so the null hypothesis was rejected.

Preliminary results of t-test paired samples statistics of BV2_AVG and ROA3_AVG data were that the three-year securities average book price (M = 27.83, SD = 6.78) was significantly more important than the three-year securities average Return-on-Assets (ROA) (M = 2.75, SD = 0.80), $t(15)$ = 14.47, p < .05, d = 3.62. The paired sample correlation result was -0.138, p = 0.610. The results of this analysis indicated a resultant tested p-value that was significant at less than .05, so the null hypothesis was rejected.

CIK 3068 was the only sample firm that was a low market-to-book value firm (threshold - the market-to-book ratio is a ratio less than 1:1). Therefore, in the practitioner sense of the study at hand, with only one firm in the 16 firm sample with a low market-to-book price, there was no practical means of analyzing the sample with respect to Hypothesis 1. There was a dearth of data from the sample for analysis in this respect.

Stage 2 of the Study

The second stage of the study for Hypothesis 1, as described in Chapter Three, involved an injection of contrived assets, or what has been more commonly known as synthetic, paired assets. The synthetic asset was a study created, theoretically frictionless derivative payout that occurred when the debt ratio of a firm in the sample of 16 firms reflected a debt-ratio higher than 60%. Since all of the firms in the sample of 16 firms were characterized by debt-ratios of more than 60%, the stage two analyses involved the addition of the derivative to the total assets of each firm in the sample 16 firms' most recent balance sheets (year 2012) such that the debt-ratio was brought back to the 50% debt-ratio currently reported by most American firms (see Appendix L for data analyzed). Only the 2012 debt was used in order to reflect Treynor's findings from the literature review of Chapter Two above.

Results of the two-tailed t-test paired samples statistics of a sample firm's derivative adjusted Adj_BV2_2012 (Book Price) and MP1_2012 data were that the 2012 annual report adjusted book price ($M = 71.85$, $SD = 25.24$) was significantly more important than the firm's 2012 securities market price ($M = 43.71$, $SD = 14.84$), $t(15) = 6.90$, p < .05, $d = 1.72$. The paired sample correlation result was 0.789, p < .05. The results of this analysis indicated a resultant tested p-value that was significant at less than .05, so the null hypothesis was rejected.

Results of the two-tailed t-test paired samples statistics of a sample firm's derivative adjusted Adj_BV2_2012 (Book Price) and ROA3_2012 data were that the 2012 annual report adjusted book price ($M = 71.85$, $SD = 25.24$) was significantly more important than the firm's 2012 Return-on-Assets (ROA) ($M = 2.77$, $SD = 0.64$), $t(15) = 10.84$, p < .05, $d = 2.71$. The paired sample correlation result was -0.378, p = 0.149. The results of this analysis indicated a resultant tested *p*-value that was significant at less than .05, so the null hypothesis was rejected.

Results of the two-tailed *t*-test paired samples statistics of a sample firm's derivative adjusted Adj_BV2_2012 (Book Price) and ROA3_AVG data were that the 2012 annual report adjusted book price ($M = 71.85$, $SD = 25.24$) was significantly more important than the firm's three-year average Return-on-Assets (ROA) ($M = 2.75$, $SD = 0.80$), $t(15) = 10.83$, p < .05, $d = 2.71$. The paired sample correlation result was -0.349, p = 0.185. The results of this analysis indicated a resultant tested *p*-value that was significant at less than .05, so the null hypothesis was rejected.

Results of the two-tailed *t*-test paired samples statistics of a sample firm's ROA3_AVG and the firm's adjusted Adj_NTRFP4_2012 (market-to-book) data were that the firm's three-year average Return-on-Assets (ROA) ($M = 2.75$, $SD = 0.80$) was significantly more important than the firm's 2012 annual report adjusted market-to-book price (MVBV) ($M = 0.63$, $SD = 0.19$), $t(15) = 12.14$, p < .05, $d = 3.03$. The paired sample correlation result was 0.606, p < .05. The results of this analysis indicated a resultant tested *p*-value that was significant at less than .05, so the null hypothesis was rejected.

With regard to more advanced theoretical testing, such as regression studies or measures of association between the variables, since the sample firm's ROA3_AVG and the firm's adjusted Adj_NTRFP4_2012 two-tailed *t*-test paired samples analysis included the paired samples correlation of 0.606 (an upper-strength, moderate, positive correlation), which has been commonly accepted as being identical to the considerably more intensive Pearson correlation coefficient, this result obviated the need to perform a Pearson correlation analysis. Although an *F*-test multivariate regression was planned for these data for Hypothesis 1, three years of data points would have been necessary for each variable for all of the analyses examined but only the current sample firms' adjusted Adj_NTRFP4_2012 (market-to-book) and Adj_BV2_2012 (Book Price) were really applicable (in order for the a derivative pay-out to make sense for asset adjustment in real-time), thus the use of a full regression analysis was not indicated for Hypothesis 1. Only 2012 debt associated figures were used in order to reflect Treynor's findings from the literature review of Chapter Two above. However, a rudimentary ANOVA of MP1_2012, Adj_BV2_2012, ROA3_2012, Adj_NTRFP4_2012, and Amt_Deriv_needed did indicate that $F(4, 75) = 13.57, p < .05$. The results of this analysis indicated a resultant tested *p*-value that was significant at less than .05, so the null hypothesis was rejected.

Since the *p*-value was virtually (for the *t*-tests and the ANOVA) *zero*, which was far less statistically speaking than the required test parameter of $p < .05$, the coefficient of correlation was found to be high and very significantly different from *zero*. Further, since the preceding theoretical ROA3_AVG and Adj_NTRFP4_2012 analysis was in effect a direct analysis and examination of Hypothesis 1, such that both constructs were directly examined, and the paired samples test *p*-value was less than .05, the null hypothesis was rejected.

Hypothesis 2

$H_0 2$: There is no relationship between high market-to-book value (threshold - the market-to-book ratio is a ratio of 1:1 or more) publicly-traded U.S. electric utility companies and their 3-year annualized average return on assets.

$H_1 2$: There is a relationship between high market-to-book value (threshold - the market-to-book ratio is a ratio of 1:1 or more) publicly-traded U.S. electric utility companies and their 3-year annualized average return on assets.

The data of market price and book price per share, when combined into MVBV for this study, already reflected predominantly high market-to-book values for the firms in the 16 firm sample (threshold - the market-to-book ratio is a ratio of 1:1 or more, which could not have been known until the data were collected and analyzed). There was no use of derivatives or other manipulations for the aggregated data used in the analysis for Hypothesis 2 (for data analyzed, see Appendices G and H).

Results of the two-tailed t-test paired samples statistics of a sample firm's ROA3_AVG and the firm's NTRFP4_2010 (market-to-book) data were that the firm's three-year average Return-on-Assets (ROA) ($M = 2.75$, $SD = 0.80$) was significantly more important than the firm's 2010 annual report market-to-book price (MVBV) ($M = 1.45$, $SD = 0.54$), $t(15) = 5.64$, p < .05, $d = 1.41$. The paired sample correlation result was 0.090, $p = 0.740$. The results of this analysis indicated a resultant tested p-value that was significant at less than .05, so the null hypothesis was rejected.

Results of the two-tailed t-test paired samples statistics of a sample firm's

ROA3_AVG and the firm's NTRFP4_2011 (market-to-book) data were that

the firm's three-year average Return-on-Assets (ROA) ($M = 2.75$, $SD = 0.80$) was

significantly more important than the firm's 2011 annual report market-to-book price

(MVBV) ($M = 1.61$, $SD = 0.67$), $t(15) = 4.42$, p < .05, $d = 1.10$. The paired sample

correlation result was 0.020, $p = 0.940$. The results of this analysis indicated a resultant

tested p-value that was significant at less than .05, so the null hypothesis was rejected.

Results of the two-tailed t-test paired samples statistics of a sample firm's

ROA3_AVG and the firm's NTRFP4_2012 (market-to-book) data were that the firm's

three-year average Return-on-Assets (ROA) ($M = 2.75$, $SD = 0.80$) was significantly

more important than the firm's 2012 annual report market-to-book price (MVBV) ($M =$

1.47, $SD = 0.30$), $t(15) = 7.17$, p < .05, $d = 1.79$. The paired sample correlation result was

0.445, p = 0.084. The results of this analysis indicated a resultant tested p-value that was

significant at less than .05, so the null hypothesis was rejected.

Results of the two-tailed t-test paired samples statistics of a sample firm's three-

year ROA3_AVG and the firm's three-year NTRFP4_AVG (market-to-book) data were

that the firm's three-year average Return-on-Assets (ROA) ($M = 2.75$, $SD = 0.80$) was

significantly more important than the firm's three-year annual report market-to-book

price (MVBV) ($M = 1.52$, $SD = 0.42$), $t(15) = 5.90$, p < .05, $d = 1.47$. The paired sample

correlation result was 0.156, p = 0.563. The results of this analysis indicated a resultant

tested p-value that was significant at less than .05, so the null hypothesis was rejected.

In the analysis of the three-year data points for the three years of data from all 16 sample firms, by year to average MVBV and by average to average MVBV,

there was a positive correlation at less than the study's level of significance of $p < 0.05$.

There was no need for the use of the Pearson's r correlation analysis to operationalize the

constructs of the second set of hypotheses because the two-tailed t-test paired samples

analyses' results included the paired samples correlation. An F-test multivariate

regression was not planned for the data for Hypothesis 2. Since the preceding theoretical

tests culminated with the ROA3_AVG and NTRFP4_AVG analysis, which was a direct

analysis of Hypothesis 2, such that both constructs were directly examined, and the

paired samples test p-value was less than .05, the null hypothesis was rejected.

Hypothesis 3

$H_0 3$: There is no relationship between a publicly-traded U.S. electric utility

company leveraged above 60% and a high market-to-book value publicly-traded U.S.

electric utility company.

$H_1 3$:There is a relationship between a publicly-traded U.S. electric utility

company leveraged above 60% and a high market-to-book value publicly-traded U.S.

electric utility company.

Stage 1 of the Study

A multiple regression analysis (for data used in the following analyses, see

Appendices E, F, G, H, I, and J) was conducted predicting the sample firms' three-year

average market-to-book (NTRFP4_AVG) from the variables of three-year average

market price of the sample firms' securities (MP1_AVG), three-year average book price per share of the sample firms (BV2_AVG), and the three-year average Return-on-Assets (ROA3_AVG). The regression was significant, $F(3, 12) = 33.41$, $p < .05$, $R^2 = .89$. Of the predictors investigated, both the three-year average market price of the sample firms' securities (MP1_AVG) ($\beta = 1.47$, $t(15) = 9.87$, $p < .05$) and the three-year average book price per share of the sample firms (BV2_AVG) ($\beta = -1.137$, $t(15) = -7.57$, $p < .05$) were significant. The three-year average Return-on-Assets (ROA3_AVG) ($\beta = -.115$, $t(15) = -1.155$, $p > .05$) was not a significant predictor of the three-year average market-to-book (NTRFP4_AVG). The results of this analysis indicated a resultant tested p-value that was significant at less than .05 so the null hypothesis was rejected.

A multivariate analysis of covariance (MANCOVA) was conducted such that the dependent variables were NTRFP4_AVG and CMVCP5_AVG (the scale weight variable was CMC6_AVG), the independent variables were MP1_AVG, BV2_AVG, and ROA3_AVG, and the covariant control variables were the scale variable of *beta* (calculated from the CAPM for each firm), the categorical variable of company market capitalization (small, medium, large), and the remainder of asset impairment (assumed to be a constant of 100% since the sample firms were all legally obligated by the SEC and SOX to legally report in the annual reports all debt, which was already calculated in the firm debt-ratios – no extraneous debt was found in the financials). For the results regarding continuous variable information, the average sample firm was high market-to-book ($M = 1.51$, $SD = 0.42$), the scale weight was fully capitalized ($M = 11,126,622,723$,

SD = 16,747,489,740), and the covariates were *beta* (M = 0.87, SD = 0.24), categorical firm size of medium (M = 2.44, SD = 0.51), and the impairment remainder was a constant at 100% for all 16 firms in the sample. For the predictor variable correlations, ROA3_AVG was weak (MP1_AVG = -.278, BV2_AVG = .299), MP1_AVG was inconsistent (ROA3_AVG = -.278, BV2_AVG = -.773), and BV2_AVG was inconsistent (ROA3_AVG = .299, MP1_AVG = -.773). The covariance correlations were inconsistently positively or negatively correlated, but numerically five places from zero in either direction such that for all intents and purposes, statistically speaking, those correlations were clustered about the zero value (but were not zero) and thus were insignificant. The tests of between-subjects effects for the corrected model were NTRFP4_AVG (Type III Sum of Squares = 2.652, Mean Square = .177) and CMVCP5_AVG (Type III Sum of Squares = 109.185, Mean Square = 7.279). When the covariant variables were withdrawn and the model was re-run, there was no significant change in the above values, which practically indicated that the control variables' actual usage had no effect upon the MANCOVA.

An examination of the debt-ratio of the most recent balance sheet was of the financials from the firms in the 16 firm sample's 2012 annual reports from the online EDGAR database. The data table for those data was depicted in Appendix M.

Stage 2 of the Study

A multiple regression analysis (for data analyzed, see Appendix N) was conducted predicting the dependent variable of the three-year sample firms' MVBV

NTRFP4_2012_AVG from the predictor variables of the three-year sample

firms' market price MP1_AVG, the three-year sample firms' book price per share

BV2_AVG, the 2012 sample firms' actual debt ratio 2012_debt_ratio, the 2012 sample

firms' actual total debt 2012_debt, and the 2012 sample firms' actual total assets. The

regression was significant, $F(5, 10) = 94.76$, $p < 0.05$, $R^2 = .98$. Of the predictors

investigated, market price MP1_AVG ($\beta = 1.163$, $t(10) = 13.60$, $p < .05$), book price

BV2_AVG ($\beta = -.927$, $t(10) = -12.47$, $p < .05$), the total debt 2012_debt ($\beta = -.2.72$, $t(10)$

$= -3.75$, $p < .05$), and the total assets ($\beta = 2.95$, $t(10) = 4.14$, $p < .05$) were significant.

The predictor debt ratio 2012_debt_ratio ($\beta = 0.05$, $t(10) = 0.62$, $p > .05$) was not a

significant predictor of MVBV NTRFP4_2012. The residual Durbin-Watson test result

was $d = 1.87$. The results of a rudimentary ANOVA of the sample variables of

NTRFP4_2012_AVG, MP1_AVG, BV2_AVG, 2012_debt_ratio, 2012_debt, and

2012_assets did indicate that $F (5, 10) = 94.76$, $R^2 = 0.98$, $p < .05$. The results outputs of

the multiple regression and the accompanying ANOVA were depicted in Figures 1-5

below. The results of these analyses indicated a resultant tested p-value that was

significant at less than .05, so the null hypothesis was rejected.

141

Figure 1

Hypothesis 3 Multiple Regression Analytical Model Summary Results

Model Summary[b]

Model	R	R Square	Adjusted R Square	Std. Error of the Estimate	Change Statistics					Durbin-Watson
					R Square Change	F Change	df1	df2	Sig. F Change	
1	.990[a]	.979	.969	.07404	.979	94.760	5	10	.000	1.871

a. Predictors: (Constant), BV2_AVG, Debt_ratio_2012, Assets_2012, MP1_AVG, Debt_2012

b. Dependent Variable: NTRFP4_AVG

Figure 2

Hypothesis 3 Multiple Regression ANOVA Summary Results

ANOVA[a]

Model		Sum of Squares	df	Mean Square	F	Sig.
1	Regression	2.597	5	.519	94.760	.000[b]
	Residual	.055	10	.005		
	Total	2.652	15			

a. Dependent Variable: NTRFP4_AVG

b. Predictors: (Constant), BV2_AVG, Debt_ratio_2012, Assets_2012, MP1_AVG, Debt_2012

Figure 3

Hypothesis 3 Multiple Regression Coefficients Summary Results

Model		Unstandardized Coefficients		Standardized Coefficients	t	Sig.	Correlations			Collinearity Statistics	
		B	Std. Error	Beta			Zero-order	Partial	Part	Tolerance	VIF
1	(Constant)	1.175	.485		2.423	.036					
	Debt_2012	-5.565E-011	.000	-2.717	-3.749	.004	.623	-.764	-.170	.004	254.092
	Assets_2012	4.115E-011	.000	2.952	4.144	.002	.665	.795	.188	.004	245.567
	Debt_ratio_2012	.004	.007	.049	.620	.549	-.232	.192	.028	.335	2.988
	MP1_AVG	.039	.003	1.163	13.601	.000	.609	.974	.618	.283	3.539
	BV2_AVG	-.058	.005	-.927	-12.467	.000	-.012	-.969	-.567	.374	2.677

a. Dependent Variable: NTRFP4_AVG

Figure 4

Hypothesis 3 Multiple Regression Collinearity Summary Results

Collinearity Diagnostics[a]

Model	Dimension	Eigenvalue	Condition Index	Variance Proportions					
				(Constant)	Debt_ 2012	Assets 2012	Debt_ratio _2012	MP1_AVG	BV2_AVG
1	1	5.142	1.000	.00	.00	.00	.00	.00	.00
	2	.785	2.559	.00	.00	.00	.00	.00	.00
	3	.055	9.672	.01	.00	.00	.01	.16	.06
	4	.013	20.251	.00	.00	.00	.00	.72	.87
	5	.004	34.659	.06	.15	.17	.05	.11	.06
	6	.000	102.705	.93	.84	.83	.94	.01	.00

a. Dependent Variable: NTRFP4_AVG

Figure 5

Hypothesis 3 Multiple Regression Residual Statistics Summary Results

Residuals Statistics[a]

	Minimum	Maximum	Mean	Std. Deviation	N
Predicted Value	.9590	2.7208	1.5119	.41613	16
Residual	-.10841	.10085	.00000	.06045	16
Std. Predicted Value	-1.329	2.905	.000	1.000	16
Std. Residual	-1.464	1.362	.000	.816	16

a. Dependent Variable: NTRFP4_AVG

Results of the two-tailed *t*-test paired samples statistics of a sample firm's current debt-ratio Debt_ratio_2012 and the firm's three-year average unadjusted MVBV NTRFP4_AVG (market-to-book) data were that the sample firms' current debt-ratio

Debt_ratio_2012 ($M = 69.97$, $SD = 4.70$) was significantly more important

than the sample firms' three-year average unadjusted MVBV NTRFP4_AVG (market-to-

book) ($M = 1.51$, $SD = 0.42$), $t(15) = 56.82$, $p < .05$, $d = 14.2$. The paired sample

correlation result was -0.232, $p > 0.05$. Only 2012 debt associated figures were used in

order to reflect Treynor's findings from the literature review of Chapter Two above. The

results of this analysis indicated a resultant tested p-value that was significant at less than

.05, so the null hypothesis was rejected.

In the analysis of the data points for the data from all 16 sample firms, by year to

average MVBV and by average variable to average MVBV, there was a positive

correlation at less than the study's level of significance of $p < 0.05$. There was no need

for the use of the Pearson's r correlation analysis to operationalize the constructs of the

third set of hypotheses because the two-tailed t-test paired samples analysis included the

paired samples correlation. Although an F-test multivariate regression was planned for

these data for Hypothesis 3, three years of data points would have been necessary for

each variable examined but only the current debt-ratio was actually applicable in a

practitioner sense to this analysis (since only the current debt-ratio was applicable), thus

the use of regression analysis was conducted to look for spurious variables but was

actually not needed based upon the observed results of the analysis. The 2012 debt

associated figures were used in order to reflect Treynor's findings from the literature

review of Chapter Two above. A rudimentary ANOVA of NTRFP4_AVG, 2012_debt,

2012_assets, 2012_debt_ratio, and BV2_AVG did indicate that $F (5, 10) = 94.76$, $R^2 =$

0.98, $p < .05$. Since the preceding Debt_ratio_2012 and NTRFP4_AVG

analysis was a direct analysis of Hypothesis 3, such that both constructs were directly

examined, and the paired samples test and ANOVA p-values were each less than .05, the

null hypothesis was rejected.

Hypothesis 4

$H_0 4$: There is no relationship between the use of a derivative induced, synthetic

asset treatment to move a publicly-traded U.S. electric utility company from a high

market-to-book value to a low market-to-book value.

$H_1 4$: There is a relationship between the use of a derivative induced, synthetic

asset treatment to move a publicly-traded U.S. electric utility company from a high

market-to-book value to a low market-to-book value.

A partial multiple regression using Fama-French analytical techniques was

performed using the three-year average processed data shown in Appendix O. The actual

equation used to perform the multiple regression was the complete Fama-French multiple

regression equation, which was described as equation 3.3 in Chapter Three (Fama &

French, 2004, p. 38), which is depicted below as equation 4.1.

$$E(R_{it}) - R_{ft} = \beta_0 + \beta_{iM}[E(R_{Mt}) - R_{ft}] + \beta_{is}E(SMB_t) + \beta_{ih}E(HML_t)$$

Equation 4.1

The three-year average $((R_{it}) - (R_{ft}))$ excess security return for the firms in the sample, for

the years 2010, 2011, 2012, was calculated from the data in the appendices and from the

sample firms' annual reports. The remaining three variables' data of $E(R_{Mt}) - R_{ft}$,

$E(SMB_t)$, and $E(HML_t)$ were downloaded from the Ken French online site for data use that was discussed in Chapter Three (see Appendix O).

The partial multiple regression was conducted to only determine the *betas* of the β_{iM}, β_{is}, and β_{ih}, variable*s (β_0* was implied in the regression equation's right side and was also determined) shown in the complete Fama-French multiple regression Equation 4.1 above to then calculate the equation's j-index rectifier and to confirm the amount of derivative payout necessary to move each of the 16 sample firms' debt-ratios back to the 50% guideline reported by American firms, discussed in earlier chapters above. The regression was significant, $F(3, -1) = -.4501$, $p < .05$, $R^2 = 39.04$. The results of this analysis indicated a resultant tested p-value that was significant at less than .05, so the null hypothesis was rejected. The *betas* were determined to be β_0 (intercept) = -72, $\beta_{iM} = 7.25$, $\beta_{is} = -2.5$, and $\beta_{ih} = 0$. These *betas* were then used as data plugs in Equation 4.1 to determine the *j*-index rectifier value (to make both sides of the equation actually equal) for each of the 16 sample firms in the 2012 sample year as though those associated firm securities were to be prospective investments (see Table 5).

Table 5

Sample of 16 coded sample firms (H0: 4 Fama-French Regression-Equated Results)

CIK	(should be) excess ret 2012	what it is (2012 result)	2012 j-index
2224	7.98	44.7275	-36.748
6160	9.94	44.7275	-34.788
3068	15.48	44.7275	-29.248
0464	21.18	44.7275	-23.548
1728	19.55	44.7275	-25.178
1138	14.34	44.7275	-30.388
3308	10.75	44.7275	-33.978
2910	14.99	44.7275	-29.738
3088	15.15	44.7275	-29.578
2541	14.01	44.7275	-30.718
9819	14.99	44.7275	-29.738
2208	13.85	44.7275	-30.878
2903	10.59	44.7275	-34.138
7877	17.92	44.7275	-26.808
6863	16.78	44.7275	-27.948
7052	7.98	44.7275	-36.748

A bivariate regression analysis was performed upon the results' manually calculated *j*-index previously calculated independent variable of CMVCP5_2012 and the dependent variable multiple regression resultant study-recalculated j-index

(from Table 5 above). The regression was significant, $F(1, 14) = 172{,}847.215$, $p < .05$, R^2 = 1.00. The predictor CMVCP5_2012 ($\beta = -1.0$, $t(14) = -415.749$, $p < .05$) was significant. Although these results were significant, the results would not be used to calculate the amount of synthetic derivative payment necessary to bring a firm leveraged above 60% back to the reported 50% debt-ratio since the calculation was coincidentally determined by calculations already used previously in the Chapter Four data analysis above. The results of this analysis indicated a resultant tested p-value that was significant at less than .05, so the null hypothesis was rejected.

A second multiple regression analysis (for data analyzed, see Appendices L and M) was conducted predicting the MVBV dependent variable of Adj_NTRFP4_2012 from the predictor variables of 2012 sample firms' market price MP1_2012, the sample firms' actual 2012 debt ratio Debt_ratio_2012, the actual amount of synthetic asset derivative payout amount needed to move each sample firm levered above 60% back to the reported 50% guideline Amt_Deriv_needed, and the adjusted 2012 sample firms' book value taking into account the respective derivative payouts for each sample firm Adj_BV2_2012. The regression was significant, $F(4, 11) = 26.15$, $p < 0.05$, $R^2 = .91$. The results outputs of the second multiple regression and the accompanying ANOVA were depicted in Figures 6-10 below. The results of this analysis indicated a resultant tested p-value that was significant at less than .05, so the null hypothesis was rejected. Of the predictors investigated, both the 2012 market price MP1_2012 ($\beta = 1.50$, $t(11) = 7.79$, p

< .05) and the 2012 sample firms' adjusted book value Adj_BV2_2012 (β = -1.59, $t(11)$ = -6.85, $p < .05$) were significant. Both the actual 2012 debt ratio Debt_ratio_2012 ($\beta = 0.09$, $t(11) = .625$, $p > .05$) and 2012 sample firms' relevered Amt_Deriv_needed ($\beta = 0.00$, $t(11) = .000$, $p > .05$) variables were not significant predictors of MVBV Adj_NTRFP4_2012. The residual Durbin-Watson test result was d = 1.77. The results of the associated rudimentary ANOVA of the sample variables of Adj_NTRFP4_2012_AVG, MP1_2012, Adj_BV2_2012, 2012_debt_ratio, and Deriv_needed indicated that $F(4, 11) = 26.15$, $R^2 = 0.91$, $p < .05$. The results of this analysis indicated a resultant tested p-value that was significant at less than .05, so the null hypothesis was rejected.

Figure 6

Hypothesis 4 Multiple Regression Analytical Model Summary Results

Model Summary[b]

Model	R	R Square	Adjusted R Square	Std. Error of the Estimate	Change Statistics					Durbin-Watson
					R Square Change	F Change	df1	df2	Sig. F Change	
1	.951[a]	.905	.870	.06712	.905	26.149	4	11	.000	1.769

a. Predictors: (Constant), MP1_2012, Debt_ratio_2012, Amt_Deriv_needed, Adj_BV2_2012

b. Dependent Variable: Adj_NTRFP4_2012

Figure 7

Hypothesis 4 Multiple Regression ANOVA Summary Results

ANOVA[a]

Model		Sum of Squares	df	Mean Square	F	Sig.
1	Regression	.471	4	.118	26.149	.000[b]
	Residual	.050	11	.005		
	Total	.521	15			

a. Dependent Variable: Adj_NTRFP4_2012

b. Predictors: (Constant), MP1_2012, Debt_ratio_2012, Amt_Deriv_needed, Adj_BV2_2012

Figure 8

Hypothesis 4 Multiple Regression Coefficients Summary Results

Coefficients[a]

Model	Unstandardized Coefficients		Standardized Coefficients	t	Sig.	Correlations			Collinearity Statistics	
	B	Std. Error	Beta			Zero-order	Partial	Part	Tolerance	VIF
(Constant)	.413	.366		1.131	.282					
Debt_ratio_2012	.003	.005	.085	.625	.545	-.611	.185	.058	.469	2.130
1 Amt_Deriv_needed	1.001E-013	.000	.000	.000	1.000	-.322	.000	.000	.538	1.859
Adj_BV2_2012	-.012	.002	-1.590	-6.847	.000	-.363	-.900	-.637	.160	6.233
MP1_2012	.019	.002	1.504	7.787	.000	.252	.920	.724	.232	4.310

a. Dependent Variable: Adj_NTRFP4_2012

151

Figure 9

Hypothesis 4 Multiple Regression Collinearity Summary Results

Collinearity Diagnostics[a]

Model	Dimension	Eigen value	Condition Index	Variance Proportions				
				(Constant)	Debt_ratio 2012	Amt_Deriv _needed	Adj_BV2 2012	MP1_ 2012
1	1	4.514	1.000	.00	.00	.01	.00	.00
	2	.399	3.363	.00	.00	.56	.00	.00
	3	.068	8.145	.01	.01	.20	.04	.14
	4	.018	15.821	.00	.00	.21	.56	.42
	5	.001	67.678	.99	.99	.02	.40	.44

a. Dependent Variable: Adj_NTRFP4_2012

Figure 10

Hypothesis 4 Multiple Regression Residual Statistics Summary Results

Residuals Statistics[a]

	Minimum	Maximum	Mean	Std. Deviation	N
Predicted Value	.2719	1.0770	.6306	.17723	16
Residual	-.08425	.14814	.00000	.05747	16
Std. Predicted Value	-2.024	2.519	.000	1.000	16
Std. Residual	-1.255	2.207	.000	.856	16

a. Dependent Variable: Adj_NTRFP4_2012

Results of the two-tailed *t*-test paired samples statistics of a sample firm's 2012 debt-ratio Debt_ratio_2012 and the sample firm's 2012 MVBV adjusted for the added asset value of the appropriate synthetic asset derivative payout per firm

Adj_NTRFP4_2012 (market-to-book) data were that the firms'

Debt_ratio_2012 ($M = 69.97$, $SD = 4.70$) was significantly more important than the

firms' Adj_NTRFP4_2012 ($M = .63$, $SD = 0.19$), $t(15) = 57.54$, p $< .05$, $d = 14.39$. The

paired sample correlation result was -0.611, p $< .05$. The results of this analysis indicated

a resultant tested p-value that was significant at less than .05, so the null hypothesis was

rejected.

In the analysis of the data points for the data from all 16 sample firms, by year to

year variable in the bivariate regression, by 2012 annual variables in the second multiple

regression, and by annual variables in the ANOVA, there was a positive correlation at

less than the study's level of significance of $p < 0.05$. There was no need for the use of

the Pearson's r correlation analysis to operationalize the constructs of the fourth set of

hypotheses because the two-tailed t-test paired samples analysis included the paired

samples correlation. However, a rudimentary ANOVA of Adj_NTRFP4_2012,

MP1_2012, 2012_debt_ratio, Deriv_needed, and Adj_BV2_2012 did indicate that $F (4,$

$11) = 26.17$, $R^2 = 0.91$, $p < .05$. Since the preceding theoretical Debt_ratio_2012 and

Adj_NTRFP4_2012 analysis was a direct analysis of Hypothesis 4, such that both

constructs were directly examined, and the ANOVA and paired samples t-test p-values

were each less than .05, the null hypothesis was rejected.

Hypothesis 5

H_05: There is no relationship between a publicly-traded U.S. electric utility

company's non-traditional, relative pricing, a study derived computer model's variant pricing of the company, and the company's market capitalization.

$H_1$5: There is a relationship between a publicly-traded U.S. electric utility company's non-traditional, relative pricing, a study derived computer model's variant pricing of the company, and the company's market capitalization.

A multiple regression analysis (see data analyzed in Appendix P) was conducted predicting the j-index dependent variable of the 2012 sample firms' security desirability by investors j-index_2012 from the predictor variables of the 2012 sample firms' study-adjusted MVBV non-traditional, relative pricing Adj_NTRFP4_2012, the 2012 sample firms' practitioner derived actual, annual return CMVCP5_2012, and the 2012 actual dollar amount of the sample firms' market capitalization CMC6_2012. The regression was significant, $F(3, 12) = 56,409.50$, $p < 0.05$, $R^2 = 1.00$. The results of this analysis indicated a resultant tested p-value that was significant at less than .05, so the null hypothesis was rejected. Of the predictors investigated, only the 2012 annual return CMVCP5_2012 ($\beta = -.997$, $t(12) = -273.55$, $p < .05$) was significant. The results outputs of the multiple regression and the accompanying ANOVA were depicted in Figures 11-15 below. Both the non-traditional, relative pricing Adj_NTRFP4_2012 ($\beta = 0.003$, $t(12) = 1.18$, $p > .05$) and amount of the sample firms' market capitalization CMC6_2012 ($\beta = -0.003$, $t(12) = -.75$, $p > .05$) variables were not significant. The multiple regression's residual analysis Durbin-Watson test d result was of $d = 1.47$.

Figure 11

Hypothesis 5 Multiple Regression Analytical Model Summary Results

Model Summary[b]

Model	R	R Square	Adjusted R Square	Std. Error of the Estimate	Change Statistics					Durbin-Watson
					R Square Change	F Change	df1	df2	Sig. F Change	
1	1.000[a]	1.000	1.000	.036224	1.000	56409.503	3	12	.000	1.468

a. Predictors: (Constant), CMC6_2012, Adj_NTRFP4_2012, CMVCP5_2012

b. Dependent Variable: j_index_2012

Figure 12

Hypothesis 5 Multiple Regression ANOVA Summary Results

ANOVA[a]

Model		Sum of Squares	df	Mean Square	F	Sig.
1	Regression	222.063	3	74.021	56409.503	.000[b]
	Residual	.016	12	.001		
	Total	222.079	15			

a. Dependent Variable: j_index_2012

b. Predictors: (Constant), CMC6_2012, Adj_NTRFP4_2012, CMVCP5_2012

Figure 13

Hypothesis 5 Multiple Regression Coefficients Summary Results

Coefficients[a]

Model		Unstandardized Coefficients		Standardized Coefficients	t	Sig.	Correlations			Collinearity Statistics	
		B	Std. Error	Beta			Zero-order	Partial	Part	Tolerance	VIF
1	(Constant)	-44.718	.056		-799.746	.000					
	Adj_NTRFP4_2012	.067	.057	.003	1.178	.262	.446	.322	.003	.781	1.281
	CMVCP5_2012	-.995	.004	-.997	-273.553	.000	-1.000	-1.000	-.665	.445	2.247
	CMC6_2012	-8.880E-013	.000	-.003	-.754	.465	-.672	-.213	-.002	.535	1.870

a. Dependent Variable: j_index_2012

Figure 14

Hypothesis 5 Multiple Regression Collinearity Summary Results

Collinearity Diagnostics[a]

Model	Dimension	Eigen value	Condition Index	Variance Proportions			
				(Constant)	Adj_NTRFP4 _2012	CMVCP5 _2012	CMC6 2012
1	1	3.364	1.000	.00	.00	.00	.01
	2	.580	2.407	.00	.00	.01	.43
	3	.041	9.086	.13	.97	.10	.00
	4	.015	14.922	.87	.02	.89	.56

a. Dependent Variable: j_index_2012

Figure 15

Hypothesis 5 Multiple Regression Residual Statistics Summary Results

Residuals Statistics[a]

	Minimum	Maximum	Mean	Std. Deviation	N
Predicted Value	-36.83772	-23.56769	-30.63550	3.847626	16
Residual	-.057817	.089724	.000000	.032400	16
Std. Predicted Value	-1.612	1.837	.000	1.000	16
Std. Residual	-1.596	2.477	.000	.894	16

a. Dependent Variable: j_index_2012

Since the preceding multiple regression analysis was a direct analysis of Hypothesis 5, such that both constructs were directly examined, the $R^2 = 1.00$ indicated that the predictors accounted for 100% of the *j*-index variance, and the ANOVA portion of the regression results *p*-value was also less than .05 (virtually *zero* – but not *zero*), the null hypothesis was rejected.

Chapter Four Summary and Conclusions

The ROA3_AVG and Adj_NTRFP4_2012 analysis of the study's first research question was in effect a direct analysis and examination of Hypothesis 1, such that both constructs were directly examined for Research Question 1, and the paired samples test *p*-value was significant at less than .05, so the null hypothesis for Research Question 1 was rejected. There was a demonstrated relationship between low market-to-book value (threshold - the market-to-book ratio was a ratio less than 1:1) publicly traded U.S. electric utility companies and their three-year annualized average return-on-assets.

The ROA3_AVG and NTRFP4_AVG analysis of the study's second research question was a direct analysis of Hypothesis 2, such that both constructs were directly examined for Research Question 2, and the paired samples test p-value was significant at less than .05, so the null hypothesis for Research Question 2 was rejected. There was a demonstrated relationship between high market-to-book value (threshold - the market-to-book ratio is a ratio of 1:1 or more) publicly traded U.S. electric utility companies and their three-year annualized average return on assets.

The Debt_ratio_2012 and NTRFP4_AVG analysis of the study's third research question was a direct analysis of Hypothesis 3, such that both constructs were directly examined for Research Question 3, and the resultant triangulation of results of the multiple regression analysis, two-tailed t-test, and ANOVA p-values were such that each result was significant at less than .05, so the null hypothesis for Research Question 3 was rejected. There was a demonstrated relationship between a publicly traded U.S. electric utility company leveraged above 60% and a high market-to-book value publicly traded U.S. electric utility company.

The analyses regarding the amount of synthetic assets, various book values, pricing and the adjustment of MVBV analysis of the study's fourth research question was a direct analysis of Hypothesis 4, such that both constructs were directly examined for Research Question 4, and the resultant bivariate regression, second multiple regression analysis, two-tailed t-test, and ANOVA p-values were each significant at less than .05, so the null hypothesis for Research Question 4 was rejected. There was a demonstrated relationship between the use of a derivative induced, synthetic asset treatment to move a publicly traded U.S. electric utility company from a high market-to-book

value to a low market-to-book value.

The analyses, which included a multiple regression analysis of relative price

(NTRFP4), variant price CMVCP5), and market capitalization (CMC6) variables of the

study's fifth research question, were a direct analysis of Hypothesis 5, such that both

constructs were directly examined for Research Question 5, and the triangulated multiple

regression and ANOVA results p-values were each significant at less than .05, so the null

hypothesis for Research Question 5 was rejected. There was a demonstrated relationship

between a publicly traded U.S. electric utility company's non-traditional, relative pricing,

a study derived computer model's variant pricing of the company, and the company's

market capitalization.

These Chapter Four results will be enlarged upon and extensively discussed in the

following Chapter Five area concerning this study's discussion, conclusions, and

recommendations.

Chapter 5: Discussion, Conclusions, and Recommendations

Summary

Concerning the study's first research question, because the p-value was virtually (for the relevant t-tests and the ANOVA) *zero*, which was far less than the demonstrable test parameter required of $p < .05$, the coefficient of correlation was found to be high and very significantly different from *zero*. The ANOVA and the ROA3_AVG and Adj_NTRFP4_2012 analysis triangulated the results and were a confirmation of those results from Chapter 4. Further, because the theoretical ROA3_AVG and Adj_NTRFP4_2012 analysis was a direct analysis and examination of Hypothesis 1, such that both constructs were directly examined for Research Question 1 and the paired samples test p-value was significant at less than .05, the null hypothesis for Research Question 1 was rejected. There was a demonstrated relationship between low market-to-book value (threshold - the market-to-book ratio was a ratio less than 1:1) publicly-traded U.S. electric utility companies and their 3-year annualized average return-on-assets.

Concerning the study's second research question, there was a positive correlation at less than the study's level of significance of $p < 0.05$. There was no need for the use of the Pearson's r correlation analysis to operationalize the constructs of the second set of hypotheses because the two-tailed t-test paired samples analysis included the paired samples correlation. An F-test multivariate regression was not planned for the data for Hypothesis 2. The ROA3_AVG and NTRFP4_AVG variables' two-tailed t-test (which included a paired samples 2-tailed analysis resulting in a tested significance of $p < .05$)

was a direct analysis of Hypothesis 2, such that both constructs were directly examined, and the paired samples test p-value was significant at less than .05; the null hypothesis was rejected. There was a demonstrated relationship between high market-to-book value (threshold - the market-to-book ratio is a ratio of 1:1 or more) publicly-traded U.S. electric utility companies and their 3-year annualized average return on assets.

Concerning the study's third research question, there was a positive correlation at less than the study's level of significance of $p < 0.05$. There was no need for the use of the Pearson's r correlation analysis to operationalize the constructs of the third set of hypotheses because the two-tailed t-test paired samples analysis included the paired samples correlation. Although an F-test multivariate regression was planned for these data for Hypothesis 3, 3 years of data points would have been necessary for each variable examined but only the current debt-ratio was actually applicable in a practitioner sense to this analysis because of current debt needs. The 2012 debt associated figures were used in order to reflect Treynor's findings. A rudimentary ANOVA of NTRFP4_AVG, 2012_debt, 2012_assets, 2012_debt_ratio, and BV2_AVG did confirm that $F (5, 10) =$ 94.76, $R^2 = 0.98$, $p < .05$. The results of the regression analysis, ANOVA, and two-tailed t-test triangulated the results for multiple confirmation of the observation that the results were significant at $p < .05$. Because the Debt_ratio_2012 and NTRFP4_AVG analysis was a direct analysis of Hypothesis 3, such that both constructs were directly examined, and the resultant triangulation of results of the multiple regression analysis, two-tailed t-test, and ANOVA p-values were such that each result was significant at less than .05, the null hypothesis was rejected. There was a demonstrated relationship between a publicly-traded U.S. electric utility company leveraged above 60% and a high market-to-book value publicly-traded U.S. electric utility company.

Concerning the study's fourth research question, there was a positive correlation at less than the study's level of significance of $p < 0.05$. Because the preceding analyses regarding the amount of synthetic assets, various book values, pricing and the adjustment of MVBV were direct analyses of Hypothesis 4, such that both constructs were directly examined, and the resultant bivariate regression, second multiple regression analysis, two-tailed t-test, and ANOVA p-values were each significant at less than .05, the null hypothesis was rejected. There was a demonstrated relationship between the use of a derivative induced, synthetic asset treatment to move a publicly-traded U.S. electric utility company from a high market-to-book value to a low market-to-book value.

Concerning the study's fifth research question, because the multiple regression analysis was a direct analysis of Hypothesis 5, such that the constructs were directly examined regarding relative price, variant price, and market capitalization, and the $R^2 = 1.00$ indicated that the predictors accounted for 100% of the j-index variance, and the triangulated multiple regression and ANOVA results p-values were each less than .05 (virtually *zero* – but not *zero*), the null hypothesis was rejected. There was a demonstrated relationship between a publicly-traded U.S. electric utility company's nontraditional, relative pricing, a study derived computer model's variant pricing of the company, and the company's market capitalization.

Interpretation of the Findings

Research Question 1

The study's first research question was designed to examine whether company securities were underpriced compared with the same firm's ROA. The practical means of accomplishing that was the Chapter 4 analyses that involved whether there was a relationship of any type between the sample firms' MVBV (threshold – the market-to-book ratio was a ratio less than 1:1) and those same sample firms' 3-year annualized average ROA.

Stage 1 of the Study

A basic means of testing Research Question 1 was to look for any type of significant relationship between any of the variables of the 16 sample firms' market price, book price per share, and ROA. The preliminary results from the t-test paired samples analysis of the sample firms' 3-year averaged market prices compared with the sample firms' 3-year averaged per share book prices resulted in a paired sample correlation result of 0.753 where $p < .05$. The preliminary results from the t-test paired samples analysis of the sample firms' 3-year averaged market prices compared with the sample firms' 3-year averaged return on assets resulted in a paired sample correlation result of 0.077 where $p = .776$. The preliminary results from the t-test paired samples analysis of the sample firms' 3-year averaged per share book prices compared with the sample firms' 3-year averaged return on assets resulted in a paired sample correlation result of -0.138 where $p = .610$.

CIK 3068 was the only sample firm out of the 16 sample firms that was a low market-to-book value firm (threshold - the market-to-book ratio is a ratio less than 1:1). Therefore, with only one firm in the 16 firm sample with a low market-to-book price, there was no practical means of analyzing the sample with respect to Research Question 1. There was a dearth of relevant data from the sample for analysis in this respect. The goal was to find at least one of the three relationships tested among these three variables that was significant. That was accomplished with the positive relationship (0.753) between market prices and book prices, which was significant ($p < .05$), so it was then necessary to move on to Stage 2 of the hypothesis testing for Research Question 1 that would be of a theoretical nature.

Stage 2 of the Study

A theoretical means of testing Research Question 1 was to look for any type of significant relationship between any of the variables of the 16 sample firms' market price, book price per share, and ROA, that involved an injection of contrived, synthetic assets. The synthetic asset was a study-created, theoretically frictionless derivative payout that occurred when the debt ratio of a firm in the sample of 16 firms reflected a debt-ratio higher than 60%. Because all of the firms in the sample of 16 firms were characterized by debt-ratios of more than 60% (actually, the firms were all in the frame of a 60% to 80% debt-ratio), the Stage 2 analyses involved the addition of the derivative to the total assets of each firm in the sample 16 firms' most recent balance sheets (year 2012). This was done such that the debt-ratio was brought back to the 50% debt-ratio currently reported by U.S. firms.

Evidence: The results from the two-tailed *t*-test paired samples

analysis of the sample firms' 2012 derivative adjusted book prices compared with the

sample firms' 2012 market prices were that the 2012 annual report adjusted book price

($M = 71.85$, $SD = 25.24$) was significantly more important than the 2012 securities

market prices ($M = 43.71$, $SD = 14.84$), $t(15) = 6.90$, $p < .05$, $d = 1.72$.

Conclusion: The Durbin-Watson test *d* result of $d < 2$ was accepted as evidence of

a positive, serial correlation. The paired sample correlation resulted in a strong-medium

positive correlation of 0.789, which was significant ($p < .05$).

Evidence: The results from the two-tailed *t*-test paired samples analysis of the

sample firms' 2012 derivative adjusted book prices compared with the sample firms'

2012 return-on-assets were that the 2012 annual report adjusted book price ($M = 71.85$,

$SD = 25.24$) was significantly more important than the 2012 return on assets ($M = 2.77$,

$SD = 0.64$), $t(15) = 10.84$, $p < .05$, $d = 2.71$.

Conclusion: The Durbin-Watson test *d* result of $d > 2$ was accepted as evidence of

much difference in value and a negative, serial correlation. The paired sample correlation

resulted in a weak-medium negative correlation of -0.378, which was not significant ($p =$

0.149).

Evidence: The results from the two-tailed *t*-test paired samples analysis of the

sample firms' 2012 derivative adjusted book prices compared with the sample firms' 3-

year average return on assets were that the 2012 annual report adjusted book price ($M =$

71.85, $SD = 25.24$) was significantly more important than the firms' 3-year average return on assets ($M = 2.75$, $SD = 0.80$), $t(15) = 10.83$, $p < .05$, $d = 2.71$.

Conclusion: The Durbin-Watson test *d* result of $d > 2$ was accepted as evidence of much difference in value and a negative, serial correlation. The paired sample correlation resulted in a weak-medium negative correlation of -0.349, which was not significant ($p = 0.185$).

Evidence: The results from the two-tailed *t*-test paired samples analysis of the sample firms' three-year average return on assets compared with the sample firms' adjusted 2012 market-to-book price (MVBV) (Adj_NTRFP4_2012) were that the three-year average return on assets (ROA) ($M = 2.75$, $SD = 0.80$) was significantly more important than the sample firms' adjusted 2012 market-to-book price (MVBV) ($M = 0.63$, $SD = 0.19$), $t(15) = 12.14$, $p < .05$, $d = 3.03$.

Conclusion: The Durbin-Watson test *d* result of $d > 2$ should have indicated much difference in value and a negative, serial correlation. However, the paired sample correlation resulted in a strong-medium positive correlation of 0.606, which was significant ($p < .05$). The results of the Durbin-Watson test for first-order error autocorrelation that verified correlation accuracy for these hypotheses was not what was predicted, as discussed in previous chapters above, it still reinforced the magnitude assumption for the study's generalization of results from the sample to the population.

Interpretation: With regard to more advanced theoretical testing, such as regression studies or measures of association between the variables, since the two-tailed *t*-test paired samples analysis that included the paired samples correlation of 0.606 (a strong-medium positive correlation), which has been commonly accepted as being identical to the considerably more intensive Pearson correlation coefficient, this result obviated the need to perform a Pearson correlation analysis. The need for a two-tailed t-test paired samples analysis of the sample firms' market prices and the sample firms' return-on-assets was obviated for the following reason. Only the sample firms' current market-to-book of the adjusted Adj_NTRFP4_2012 (market-to-book) and the current adjusted book price of Adj_BV2_2012 were really applicable in the stage two analysis (in order for a derivative pay-out to make sense for asset adjustment in current, real-time scenario), thus the use of a full regression analysis and other tests of analysis were not indicated for Hypothesis 1. The 2012 debt associated figures were used in order to reflect Treynor's findings from the literature review of Chapter Two above. However, a rudimentary analysis of variance (ANOVA) of the variables of MP1_2012, Adj_BV2_2012, ROA3_2012, Adj_NTRFP4_2012, and Amt_Deriv_needed did indicate that $F(4, 75) = 13.57$, $p < .05$.

Interpretive Action: Since the p-value was virtually (for the relevant t-tests and the ANOVA) *zero*, which was far less statistically speaking than the test parameter of $p <$ .05, the coefficient of correlation was found to be high and very significantly different from *zero*. Addressed in previous chapters above, the ANOVA and the ROA3_AVG and Adj_NTRFP4_2012 analysis triangulated the results and were a confirmation of those results from Chapter Four. Further, since the preceding theoretical ROA3_AVG and Adj_NTRFP4_2012 analysis was in effect a direct analysis and examination of

Hypothesis 1, such that both constructs were directly examined for Research

Question 1, and the paired samples t-test p-value was significant at less than .05, the null

hypothesis for Research Question 1 was rejected. There was a demonstrated relationship

between low market-to-book value (threshold - the market-to-book ratio was a ratio less

than 1:1) publicly traded U.S. electric utility companies and their three-year annualized

average return on assets.

Research Question 2

The study's second research question was designed with the intent of examining

whether company securities were overpriced compared with the same firm's return-on-

assets (ROA). The practical means of accomplishing that was the Chapter Four analyses

that involved whether there was a relationship of any type between the sample firms'

high market-to-book value (MVBV) (threshold – the market-to-book ratio was a ratio of

1:1 or more) and those same sample firms' three-year annualized average return-on-

assets (ROA).

The data of market price and book price per share, when combined into MVBV

for this study, already reflected predominantly high market-to-book values for the firms

in the 16 firm sample (threshold - the market-to-book ratio is a ratio of 1:1 or more,

which could not have been known until the data were collected and analyzed). There was

no use of derivatives or other manipulations for the aggregated data used in the analysis

for Hypothesis 2 (for data analyzed, see Appendices G and H).

Evidence: The results of the two-tailed t-test paired samples statistics of a sample firm's ROA3_AVG and the firm's NTRFP4_2010 (market-to-book) data were

that the firm's three-year average Return-on-Assets (ROA) ($M = 2.75, SD = 0.80$) was

significantly more important than the firm's 2010 annual report market-to-book price

(MVBV) ($M = 1.45, SD = 0.54$), $t(15) = 5.64$, p $< .05$, $d = 1.41$.

Conclusion: The paired sample correlation result was 0.090, $p = 0.740$. The

Durbin-Watson test d result of $d < 2$ was accepted as evidence of a positive, serial

correlation. This was confirmed because the paired sample correlation resulted in a weak

positive correlation of 0.090, which was not significant ($p > .05$).

Evidence: Results of the two-tailed t-test paired samples statistics of a sample

firm's ROA3_AVG and the firm's NTRFP4_2011 (market-to-book) data were that the

firm's three-year average Return-on-Assets (ROA) ($M = 2.75, SD = 0.80$) was

significantly more important than the firm's 2011 annual report market-to-book price

(MVBV) ($M = 1.61, SD = 0.67$), $t(15) = 4.42$, p $< .05$, $d = 1.10$. The paired sample

correlation result was 0.020, $p = 0.940$.

Conclusion: The Durbin-Watson test d result of $d < 2$ was accepted as evidence of

a positive, serial correlation. This was confirmed but the paired sample correlation

resulted in a weak positive correlation of 0.020, which was not significant ($p > .05$).

Evidence: Results of the two-tailed t-test paired samples statistics of a sample

firm's ROA3_AVG and the firm's NTRFP4_2012 (market-to-book) data were that the

firm's three-year average Return-on-Assets (ROA) ($M = 2.75, SD = 0.80$) was

significantly more important than the firm's 2012 annual report market-to-book price

(MVBV) ($M = 1.47$, $SD = 0.30$), $t(15) = 7.17$, p < .05, $d = 1.79$.

Conclusion: The paired sample correlation result was 0.445, p = 0.084. The Durbin-Watson test d result of $d < 2$ was accepted as evidence of a positive, serial correlation. Unfortunately, the paired sample correlation resulted in a medium positive correlation of 0.445, which was not significant ($p > .05$).

Evidence: Results of the two-tailed t-test paired samples statistics of a sample firm's three-year ROA3_AVG and the firm's three-year NTRFP4_AVG (market-to-book) data were that the firm's three-year average Return-on-Assets (ROA) ($M = 2.75$, $SD = 0.80$) was significantly more important than the firm's three-year annual report market-to-book price (MVBV) ($M = 1.52$, $SD = 0.42$), $t(15) = 5.90$, p < .05, $d = 1.47$. The paired sample correlation result was 0.156, p = 0.563.

Conclusion: The Durbin-Watson test d result of $d < 2$ was accepted as evidence of a positive, serial correlation. This was confirmed even though the paired sample correlation resulted in a weak positive correlation of 0.156, which was unfortunately not significant ($p > .05$). The Durbin-Watson test results for first-order error autocorrelation that verified correlation accuracy for these hypotheses were significant, discussed in previous chapters above, and the results reinforced the magnitude assumption for the study's generalization of results from the sample to the population.

Interpretation: In the analysis of the three-year data points for the three years of data from all 16 sample firms, by year to average MVBV and by average to average MVBV, there was a positive correlation at less than the study's level of significance of p

< 0.05. There was no need for the use of the Pearson's *r* correlation analysis to operationalize the constructs of the second set of hypotheses because the two-tailed *t*-test paired samples analysis included the paired samples correlation. An *F*-test multivariate regression was not planned for Hypothesis 2 data.

Interpretive Action: The preceding ROA3_AVG and NTRFP4_AVG variables' two-tailed *t*-test (which included a paired sample 2-tailed analysis resulting in a tested significance of $p < .05$) was a direct analysis of Hypothesis 2, such that both constructs were directly examined, and the paired samples *t*-test *p*-value was less than .05, the null hypothesis was rejected. There was a demonstrated relationship between high market-to-book value (threshold - the market-to-book ratio is a ratio of 1:1 or more) publicly traded U.S. electric utility companies and their three-year annualized average return-on-assets.

Research Question 3

The study's third research question was designed with the intent of examining whether there was a relationship between firms leveraged above 60% and high market-to-book firms. Higher order examination analyses were performed and various comparisons were made reverting the sample firm debt-ratios to the 50% publicly reported by American firms. The practical means of accomplishing the leverage and MVBV study were the Chapter Four analyses that involved whether there was a relationship of any type between the sample firms' high market-to-book value (MVBV) (threshold – the market-to-book ratio was a ratio of 1:1 or more) and those same sample firms that were leveraged above 60%.

Stage 1 of the Study

A multiple regression analysis was conducted predicting the sample firms' three-year average market-to-book (NTRFP4_AVG) from the variables of three-year average market price of the sample firms' securities (MP1_AVG), three-year average book price per share of the sample firms (BV2_AVG), and the three-year average Return-on-Assets (ROA3_AVG). The regression was significant, $F(3, 12) = 33.41$, $p < .05$, $R^2 = .89$. Of the predictors investigated, both the three-year average market price of the sample firms' securities (MP1_AVG) ($\beta = 1.47$, $t(15) = 9.87$, $p < .05$) and the three-year average book price per share of the sample firms (BV2_AVG) ($\beta = -1.137$, $t(15) = -7.57$, $p < .05$) were significant. The three-year average Return-on-Assets (ROA3_AVG) ($\beta = -.115$, $t(15) = -1.155$, $p > .05$) was not a significant predictor of the three-year average market-to-book (NTRFP4_AVG).

A multivariate analysis of covariance (MANCOVA) was conducted such that the dependent variables were NTRFP4_AVG and CMVCP5_AVG (the scale weight variable was CMC6_AVG), the independent variables were MP1_AVG, BV2_AVG, and ROA3_AVG, and the covariant control variables were the scale variable of *beta* (calculated from the CAPM for each firm), the categorical variable of company market capitalization (small, medium, large), and the remainder of asset impairment (assumed to be a constant of 100% since the sample firms were all legally obligated by the SEC and SOX to legally report in the annual reports all debt, which was already calculated in the firm debt-ratios). For the results regarding continuous variable information, the average sample firm was high market-to-book ($M = 1.51$, $SD = 0.42$), the scale weight

was fully capitalized ($M = 11,126,622,723$, $SD = 16,747,489,740$), and the covariates

were *beta* ($M = 0.87$, $SD = 0.24$), categorical firm size of medium ($M = 2.44$, $SD = 0.51$),

and the impairment remainder was a constant at 100% for all 16 firms in the sample. For

the predictor variable correlations, ROA3_AVG was weak (MP1_AVG = -.278,

BV2_AVG = .299), MP1_AVG was inconsistent (ROA3_AVG = -.278, BV2_AVG = -

.773), and BV2_AVG was inconsistent (ROA3_AVG = .299, MP1_AVG = -.773). The

covariance correlations were inconsistently positively or negatively correlated, but

numerically five places from zero in either direction such that for all intents and

purposes, statistically speaking, those correlations were clustered about the *zero* value

(but were not *zero*) and thus were insignificant. The tests of between-subjects effects for

the corrected model were NTRFP4_AVG (Type III Sum of Squares = 2.652, Mean

Square = .177) and CMVCP5_AVG (Type III Sum of Squares = 109.185, Mean Square =

7.279). When the covariant variables were withdrawn and the model was re-run, there

was no significant change in the above values indicating that the control variables' usage

had no effect upon the MANCOVA.

The stage one regression was significant, $F (3, 12) = 33.41$, $p < .05$, $R^2 =$

.89. Of the predictors investigated, both the three-year average market price of the

sample firms' securities (MP1_AVG) ($\beta = 1.47$, $t(15) = 9.87$, $p < .05$) and the

three-year average book price per share of the sample firms (BV2_AVG) ($\beta = -$

1.137, $t(15) = -7.57$, $p < .05$) were significant. The meaning was that market price and book price were significant predictors and that 89% of the results were accounted for by the predictors, but that about 11% was due to other factors.

The conclusions of the stage one MANCOVA for the predictor variable correlations were, ROA3_AVG was weak (MP1_AVG = -.278, BV2_AVG = .299), MP1_AVG was inconsistent (ROA3_AVG = -.278, BV2_AVG = -.773), and BV2_AVG was inconsistent (ROA3_AVG = .299, MP1_AVG = -.773). No spurious variables were found in the MANCOVA study. Thus, the MANCOVA correlations concerning the sample firms' three-year market price, book price per share, and Return-on-Assets were either weak or inconsistent. When the covariant variables were withdrawn and the model was re-run, there was no significant change in the above values indicating that the control variables' usage had no effect upon the MANCOVA analysis.

Stage 2 of the Study

Evidence: A multiple regression analysis was conducted predicting the dependent variable of the three-year sample firms' MVBV NTRFP4_2012_AVG from the predictor variables of the three-year sample firms' market price MP1_AVG, the three-year sample firms' book price per share BV2_AVG, the 2012 sample firms' actual debt ratio 2012_debt_ratio, the 2012 sample firms' actual total debt 2012_debt, and the 2012 sample firms' actual total assets. The regression was significant, $F(5, 10) = 94.76$, $p < 0.05$, $R^2 = .98$. Of the predictors investigated, market price MP1_AVG ($\beta = 1.16$, $t(10) = 13.60$, $p < .05$), book price BV2_AVG ($\beta = -0.93$, $t(10) = -12.47$, $p < .05$), the total debt

2012_debt (β = -2.72, $t(10)$ = -3.75, p < .05), and the total assets (β = 2.95,

$t(10)$ = 4.14, p < .05) were significant. The predictor debt ratio 2012_debt_ratio (β = 0.05,

$t(10)$ = 0.62, p > .05) was not a significant predictor of MVBV NTRFP4_2012. The

multiple regression's residual Durbin-Watson test result was d = 1.87. The results of a

rudimentary ANOVA of the sample variables of NTRFP4_2012_AVG, MP1_AVG,

BV2_AVG, 2012_debt_ratio, 2012_debt, and 2012_assets did indicate that F (5, 10) =

94.76, R^2 = 0.98, p < .05.

$\quad$ *Conclusion*: The stage two multiple regression was significant, F (5, 10) = 94.76,

p < .05, R^2 = .98. Of the predictors investigated, market price (β = 1.16, $t(10)$ = 13.60, p <

.05), book price (β = -0.93, $t(10)$ = -12.47, p < .05), the total debt (β = -2.72, $t(10)$ = -

3.75, p < .05), and the total assets (β = 2.95, $t(10)$ = 4.14, p < .05) were significant. The

meaning was that market price and book price, total debt, and total assets were significant

predictors and that 98% of the results were accounted for by the predictors, but that about

2% was due to other factors. The multiple regression's Durbin-Watson test d result of d <

2 was accepted as evidence of a positive, serial correlation. This was confirmed because

the paired sample correlation resulted in a weak positive correlation of 0.156, which was

significant (p <.05). The results of the multiple regression's Durbin-Watson test for first-

order error autocorrelation that verified correlation accuracy for these hypotheses was

significant, as discussed in previous chapters above, and those results reinforced the

magnitude assumption for this study's generalization of the results from the sample to the

population.

Evidence: The results of the two-tailed *t*-test paired samples statistics of a sample firm's current debt-ratio Debt_ratio_2012 and the firm's three-year average unadjusted MVBV NTRFP4_AVG (market-to-book) data were that the sample firms' current debt-ratio Debt_ratio_2012 ($M = 69.97$, $SD = 4.70$) was significantly more important than the sample firms' three-year average unadjusted MVBV NTRFP4_AVG (market-to-book) ($M = 1.51$, $SD = 0.42$), $t(15) = 56.82$, $p < .05$, $d = 14.2$.

Conclusion: The two-tailed *t*-test Durbin-Watson test *d* result of $d > 2$ was accepted as evidence of much difference in value and a negative, serial correlation. The paired sample correlation resulted in a weak negative correlation of -0.232, which was not significant ($p > .05$).

Interpretation: In the analysis of the data points for the data from all 16 sample firms, by year to average MVBV and by average variable to average MVBV, the multiple regression's results indicated that there was a positive correlation at less than the study's level of significance of $p < 0.05$. There was no need for the use of the Pearson's *r* correlation analysis to operationalize the constructs of the third set of hypotheses because the two-tailed *t*-test paired samples analysis included the paired samples correlation. Although an *F*-test multivariate regression was planned for these data for Hypothesis 3, three years of data points would have been necessary for each variable examined but only the current debt-ratio was actually applicable in a practitioner sense to this analysis (only the current debt-ratio was applicable – three years of data were unnecessary). The 2012 debt associated figures were used in order to reflect Treynor's findings from the literature review of Chapter Two above. A rudimentary ANOVA of NTRFP4_AVG,

2012_debt, 2012_assets, 2012_debt_ratio, and BV2_AVG did confirm that $F\,(5,\,10) =$

94.76, $R^2 = 0.98$, $p < .05$. The multiple regression's Durbin-Watson test d result of $d < 2$

was accepted as evidence of a positive, serial correlation. The Durbin-Watson test results

for first-order error autocorrelation that verified correlation accuracy for these hypotheses

were significant, discussed in previous chapters above, and the results reinforced the

magnitude assumption for the study's generalization of results from the sample to the

population.

Interpretive Action: The results of the regression analysis, ANOVA, and two-

tailed t-test triangulated the results for multiple confirmation of the observation that the

results were generally significant at $p < .05$. Since the preceding Debt_ratio_2012 and

NTRFP4_AVG analysis was a direct analysis of Hypothesis 3, such that both constructs

were directly examined, and the resultant regression analysis, two-tailed t-test, and

ANOVA p-values were each less than .05, the null hypothesis was rejected. There was a

demonstrated relationship between a publicly traded U.S. electric utility company

leveraged above 60% and a high market-to-book value publicly traded U.S. electric

utility company.

Research Question 4

The study's fourth research question was designed with the intent of examining

whether there was a relationship between the use of a synthetic asset that revalued a

sample firm and the associated firm's movement from a high market-to-book to a low market-to-book value.

Evidence: The partial multiple regression to determine the *beta*-intercepts for use in the Fama-French equation was significant, $F(3, -1) = -.4501$, $p < .05$, $R^2 = 39.04$. However, the only other observation that was of note for the results from this analysis, other than being significant, was that only 39% of the results were accounted for by the predictors and about 61% was due to other factors.

Conclusion: The 39% figure was critical in this instance. However, two tools herein should not be confused. Even though a study-based Excel computer model process was used to re-orient debt in this study, since unfortunately only 39% of the results of this particular analysis were due to the predictors, then the need for an intended study-resultant computer model to forecast such *j*-indices was rendered moot and the computer model was effectively not written.

Evidence: A bivariate regression analysis was performed upon the results' manually calculated *j*-index previously calculated independent variable of CMVCP5_2012 and the dependent variable multiple regression resultant study-recalculated j-index (from Table 5 above). The regression was significant, $F(1, 14) = 172,847.215$, $p < .05$, $R^2 = 1.0$. The predictor CMVCP5_2012 ($\beta = -1.0$, $t(14) = -415.749$, $p < .05$) was significant.

Conclusion: Although these results were significant and were used to confirm the writing of and the need for the *j*-index, these results would not be used to calculate the amount of synthetic derivative payment necessary to bring a firm leveraged above 60%

back to the reported 50% debt-ratio since the calculation was coincidentally

determined by manual calculations already used previously in the Chapter Four data

analysis above.

Evidence: A second multiple regression analysis was conducted predicting the

MVBV dependent variable of Adj_NTRFP4_2012 from the predictor variables of 2012

sample firms' market price MP1_2012, the sample firms' actual 2012 debt ratio

Debt_ratio_2012, the actual amount of synthetic asset derivative payout amount needed

to move each sample firm levered above 60% back to the reported 50% guideline with

Amt_Deriv_needed, and the adjusted 2012 sample firms' book value taking into account

the respective derivative payouts for each sample firm Adj_BV2_2012. The regression

was significant, $F(4, 11) = 26.15$, $p < 0.05$, $R^2 = .91$. Of the predictors investigated, both

the 2012 market price MP1_2012 ($\beta = 1.50$, $t(11) = 7.79$, $p < .05$) and the 2012 sample

firms' adjusted book value Adj_BV2_2012 ($\beta = -1.59$, $t(11) = -6.85$, $p < .05$) were

significant. Both the actual 2012 debt ratio Debt_ratio_2012 ($\beta = 0.09$, $t(11) = .625$, $p >$

.05) and 2012 sample firms' relevered Amt_Deriv_needed ($\beta = 0.000$, $t(11) = .000$, $p >$

.05) variables were not significant predictors of MVBV Adj_NTRFP4_2012. The

residual Durbin-Watson test result was $d = 1.77$. The results of the associated

rudimentary ANOVA of the sample variables of Adj_NTRFP4_2012_AVG, MP1_2012,

Adj_BV2_2012, 2012_debt_ratio, and Deriv_needed did indicated that $F(4, 11) = 26.17$,

$R^2 = 0.91$, $p < .05$.

Conclusion: The meaning of the analysis above was that market price and book price adjusted with the use of synthetic derivatives were significant predictors

and that 91% of the results were accounted for by the predictors, but that about 9% was

due to other factors. The second multiple regression's Durbin-Watson test d result of $d <$

2 was accepted as evidence of a positive, serial correlation. The results of the multiple

regression's Durbin-Watson test for first-order error autocorrelation that verified

correlation accuracy for these hypotheses was significant, as discussed in previous

chapters above, and those results reinforced the magnitude assumption for this study's

generalization of the results from the sample to the population.

Evidence: The results of the two-tailed t-test paired samples statistics of a sample

firm's 2012 debt-ratio Debt_ratio_2012 and the sample firm's 2012 MVBV adjusted for

the added asset value of the appropriate synthetic asset derivative payout per firm

Adj_NTRFP4_2012 (market-to-book) data were that the firms' Debt_ratio_2012 ($M =$

69.97, $SD = 4.70$) was significantly more important than the firms' Adj_NTRFP4_2012

($M = .63$, $SD = 0.19$), $t(15) = 57.54$, $p < .05$, $d = 14.39$. The paired sample correlation

result was -0.611, $p < .05$.

Conclusion: The Durbin-Watson test d result of $d > 2$ was accepted as evidence of

much difference in value and a negative, serial correlation. The paired sample correlation

resulted in a strong-medium negative correlation of -0.611, which was significant ($p <$

.05). Due to the negative correlation that was significant, this analysis confirmed that as

the derivative synthetic assets were added, the market-to-book value decreased

theoretically making the associated security a better buy for investors.

Interpretation: The results of the bivariate regression, the second multiple regression analysis of adjusted MVBV from the predictors of market price, actual debt ratio, derivative payout amount needed, and the adjusted book value, and the ANOVA, generally triangulated the results for multiple confirmation of the observation that the results were significant at $p < .05$. The second multiple regression's Durbin-Watson test d result of $d < 2$ was accepted as evidence of a positive, serial correlation. The results of the multiple regression's Durbin-Watson test for first-order error autocorrelation that verified correlation accuracy for these hypotheses was significant, as discussed in previous chapters above, and those results reinforced the magnitude assumption for this study's generalization of the results from the sample to the population.

Interpretive Action: Since the preceding analyses regarding the amount of synthetic assets, various book values, pricing and the adjustment of MVBV were direct analyses of Hypothesis 4, such that both constructs were directly examined, and the resultant bivariate regression, second multiple regression analysis, and ANOVA *p*-values were each less than .05, the null hypothesis was rejected. There was a demonstrated relationship between the use of a derivative induced, synthetic asset treatment to move a publicly traded U.S. electric utility company from a high market-to-book value to a low market-to-book value.

Research Question 5

Evidence: A multiple regression analysis was conducted predicting the *j*-index dependent variable of the 2012 sample firms' security desirability by investors j-index_2012 from the predictor variables of the 2012 sample firms' study-adjusted MVBV non-traditional, relative pricing Adj_NTRFP4_2012, the 2012 sample firms' practitioner derived actual, annual return CMVCP5_2012, and the 2012 actual dollar amount of the sample firms' market capitalization CMC6_2012. The regression was significant, $F(3, 12) = 56,409.50$, $p < 0.05$, $R^2 = 1.00$. Of the predictors investigated, only the 2012 annual return variant price CMVCP5_2012 ($\beta = -.997$, $t(12) = -273.55$, $p < .05$) was significant. Both the non-traditional, relative pricing Adj_NTRFP4_2012 ($\beta = 0.003$, $t(12) = 1.178$, $p > .05$) and amount of the sample firms' market capitalization CMC6_2012 ($\beta = -0.003$, $t(12) = -.754$, $p > .05$) variables were not significant. The multiple regression's residual analysis Durbin-Watson test d result was of $d = 1.47$.

Conclusion: The results of a rudimentary ANOVA of the sample variables of Adj_NTRFP4_2012, 2012_j-index, CMVCP5_2012, and CMC6_2012 indicated that F $(3, 12) = 56,410$, $R^2 = 1.00$, $p < .05$, such that the results were significant and the predictors explained 100% of the results. The meaning was that variant price was a significant predictor of the tabulated j-index Fama-French equation valuation rectifier and that 100% of the results were accounted for by the predictors. The multiple regression's Durbin-Watson test d result of $d < 2$ was accepted as evidence of a positive, serial correlation. This was confirmed because the paired sample correlation resulted in a medium positive correlation, which was significant ($p < .05$). The results of the multiple regression's Durbin-Watson test for first-order error autocorrelation that verified correlation accuracy for these hypotheses was significant, as discussed in previous chapters above, and those results reinforced the magnitude assumption for this study's generalization of the results from the sample to the population.

Interpetive Action: Since the preceding multiple regression analysis was a direct analysis of Hypothesis 5, such that the constructs were directly examined regarding relative price, variant price, and market capitalization, and the $R^2 = 1.00$ indicated that the predictors accounted for 100% of the j-index variance, and the triangulated multiple regression and ANOVA results' p-values were each less than .05 (virtually *zero*), the null hypothesis was rejected. There was a demonstrated relationship between a publicly traded U.S. electric utility company's non-traditional, relative pricing, a study derived computer model's variant pricing of the company, and the company's market capitalization.

Action Recommendations

Concerning the study's first research question, the ANOVA and the ROA3_AVG and Adj_NTRFP4_2012 analysis triangulated the results and were a confirmation of those results from Chapter Four. However, since the theoretical stage two ROA3_AVG and Adj_NTRFP4_2012 analysis was in effect a direct analysis and examination of Hypothesis 1, such that both constructs were directly examined for Research Question 1, and the paired samples test p-value was significant at less than .05, the null hypothesis for Research Question 1 was rejected. The stage two theoretical analysis was necessary to demonstrate a relationship between low market-to-book value (threshold - the market-to-book ratio was a ratio less than 1:1) publicly traded U.S. electric utility companies and their three-year annualized average return-on-assets. The reason for this was the practically non-existent data in the sample regarding low market-to-book firms for the stage one practitioner-level analysis. For the valuable position of U.S. infrastructure mainstay, regarding the publicly traded U.S. utility companies in the study's sample, it would have been extraordinarily helpful to researchers in general, and specifically to potential, future investors, if those firm managers had been more efficient by incurring less debt and had used equity more advantageously to grow their respective firms. The confirmed ability and rationale for management's ability and the need to do this was already established in the agency theory portion of the Chapter Two literature review.

Concerning the study's second research question, the ROA3_AVG and NTRFP4_AVG variables' two-tailed t-test (which included a paired sample 2-tailed analysis resulting in a tested significance of $p < .05$) was a direct analysis of Hypothesis 2, such that both constructs were directly examined, and the paired samples test p-value was less than .05, the null hypothesis was rejected. There was a demonstrated relationship between high market-to-book value (threshold - the market-to-book ratio is a ratio of 1:1 or more) publicly traded U.S. electric utility companies and their three-year annualized average return-on-assets. Again, just as in Research Question 1, it was curious to find that as the three years of the data sampling and analysis proceeded, that the annual firm samples progressively increased in market price but steadily decreased in book price widening the gap between the two. In retrospect, this observation was originally shown in the Chapter Two literature review such that the firm market values were shown to increase as the managers of a firm increasingly assumed more debt to finance

firm growth projects. The translation of this into a more practical sense was that the

management of the sample companies obviously, of the two choices of profits sought or

firm value added, chose the avenue to guarantee their prospective future employment

such that the firm associated security prices increased. The common sense result in the

long-term (the short-term common sense implied meaning was an assurance of continued

employment for management at those firms) would obviously be MMI&II violations

such that the volume of debt would make the firm implode or make the firm ripe for

acquisition as a subsidiary by some conglomerate that might lead to eventual

reorganization and the dissolution of that same management. It would have been very

useful in a practical sense for researchers and investors alike if those managers would

have focused on adding value to the firm instead. Again, the confirmed ability and

rationale for management's ability and the need to do this was already established in the

agency theory portion of the Chapter Two literature review.

Concerning the study's third research question, the results of the regression

analysis, ANOVA, and two-tailed t-test triangulated the results for multiple confirmation

of the observation that the results were significant at $p < .05$. Since the Debt_ratio_2012

and NTRFP4_AVG analysis was a direct analysis of Hypothesis 3, such that both

constructs were directly examined, and the resultant regression analysis, two-tailed t-test,

and ANOVA p-values were each less than .05, the null hypothesis was rejected. There

was a demonstrated relationship between a publicly traded U.S. electric utility company

185

leveraged above 60% and a high market-to-book value publicly traded U.S. electric utility company.

Unfortunately, it took a second stage to this part of the study for Research Question 3 to be developed to the extent where the alternate hypothesis could be accepted. The reason was that every firm in the study's sample was leveraged far beyond the reported 50% guideline for American firms, such that the actual leverage was really between 60% and 80% for every firm in the sample. That difference represented a phenomenal amount of money in added debt for each firm amounting to billions of dollars. The original idea was that the debt difference was supposed to be hidden in the financial statements for each firm's 10-K to account for that difference in debt and could be found through the interpretation of accounting parenthetical notes or in off-balance sheet debt in other notes, but the debt was out in the open and asset impairment could not be taken in the study. Asset impairment was used instead as a constant at 100%, such that debt and reported asset values from the financials were used "as is," or "as adjusted" for various analytical tests. It would have been advantageous to researchers and conceivably to investors if the associated firms' management would have pursued instead a value philosophy that would doubly solve both issues by dovetailing the book price to meet the market price and to reduce the use of cheap debt that skewed those sample firm financials examined in exchange for the use of the more expensive equity already discussed. Once again, the confirmed ability and rationale for management's ability and the need to do this was already established in the agency theory portion of the Chapter Two literature review.

Concerning the study's fourth research question, since the preceding analyses regarding the amount of synthetic assets, various book values, pricing and the adjustment of MVBV were direct analyses of Hypothesis 4, such that both constructs were directly examined, and the resultant bivariate regression, second multiple regression analysis, two-tailed t-test, and ANOVA p-values were each less than .05, the null hypothesis was rejected. There was a demonstrated relationship between the use of a derivative induced, synthetic asset treatment to move a publicly traded U.S. electric utility company from a high market-to-book value to a low market-to-book value.

If it were assumed that a low market-to-book value firm's security was a better buy for a prospective investor than a high market-to-book value firm's security, it became a sad day in the world of investing such that the sample firms' financials needed to be adjusted with a synthetic derivative payout just to make those firms' securities look more attractive to investors. However, that was what was accomplished in this study. Someday in the real-world there may be enough of a payout from a frictionless synthetic asset to accomplish that end, but concerning these sample firms that day was not found to be the case here. Again, this was a conscious choice by firm management regarding the choice between profits and value and management ruled and governed themselves accordingly to make the decisions necessary to improve the associated firms' securities market pricing. The confirmed ability and rationale for management's ability and the need to do this was already established in the agency theory portion of the Chapter Two literature review. Previously discussed, the pursuit of value would have been a more laudatory goal.

Concerning the study's fifth research question, since the triangulated multiple regression and ANOVA results p-values were each less than .05 (virtually *zero*), the null hypothesis was rejected. There was a demonstrated relationship between a publicly traded U.S. electric utility company's non-traditional, relative pricing, a study derived computer model's variant pricing of the company, and the company's market capitalization. Even without the use of a forecasting tool such as the intended, but unwritten study-created computer model, the value that could be derived from the realization that there were relationships between relative price, variant price, and market capitalization could in future years have a strong, positive impact upon investors and the securities industry. As a former practitioner who has become intimately acquainted with the investor tools that have already been in public use by the investing community, a prospective investor could do a lot worse than to use the tenets from this study to obtain an ideological or tentative valuation of a firm, and the associated firm's equity security, by comparing the relationships demonstrated in this study between relative price, variant price, and market capitalization.

Further Study Recommendations

Concerning the study's first research question, there was a demonstrated relationship between low market-to-book value (threshold - the market-to-book ratio was a ratio less than 1:1) publicly traded U.S. electric utility companies and their three-year annualized average return-on-assets. However, it took some doing to obtain a normally distributed sample to look at the low market-to-book values. A future researcher could conceivably consider choosing a population and a sample that was already normally distributed without the use of a dozen data plugs to normalize the sample. Further, a different industry sector or a different industry altogether could be chosen that would more effectively give that future researcher more and better choices concerning the evaluation of the sample with the resultant extrapolation to the population.

Concerning the study's second research question, there was a demonstrated relationship between high market-to-book value (threshold - the market-to-book ratio is a ratio of 1:1 or more) publicly traded U.S. electric utility companies and their three-year annualized average return-on-assets. Since virtually every firm in the sample was found to be high market-to-book value, once the data had been collected and analyzed, the conclusions from those results were fairly self-evident once the analyses had been run. When a future researcher performs this same study with a different population or industry, normalcy issues aside, it would be helpful if that researcher were to look for an industry with more diversity of data to make that ensuing study more homogeneous.

Concerning the study's third research question, there was a demonstrated relationship between a publicly traded U.S. electric utility company leveraged above 60% and a high market-to-book value publicly traded U.S. electric utility company. Due to the extreme leverage found in the sample, a great deal of analyses and multiple stages were necessary to conclude the micro-study of these particular hypothetical constructs. If this study were to be performed by a future researcher on perhaps a different

sector or industry, it would be most helpful if an industry with only moderate debt-ratios

with a varied assortment of such debt in the population were to be chosen.

Concerning the study's fourth research question, there was a demonstrated

relationship between the use of a derivative induced, synthetic asset treatment to move a

publicly traded U.S. electric utility company from a high market-to-book value to a low

market-to-book value. If this study were to be performed in the future by another

researcher on perhaps a different population or sector, that researcher may find that a

synthetic asset would not be necessary to attract potential investors and that only firms

with more effective management need to be randomly chosen.

Concerning the study's fifth research question, there was a demonstrated

relationship between a publicly traded U.S. electric utility company's non-traditional,

relative pricing, a study derived computer model's variant pricing of the company, and

the company's market capitalization. If this study were to be performed in the future by

another researcher on perhaps a different population or sector, that researcher may find

that only the relative price and the market capitalization need to be examined without the

use of a contravening variant price because, as explained earlier, the sector examined by

the future researcher would not be characterized by firms with exhorbitant debt.

Social Change Implications

The short-term social change implications for this study's results and conclusions

were that these results and conclusions held the potential to positively and constructively affect social change for millions of potential investors. Millions of investors have the opportunity to use the study's tools to mitigate or minimize losses concerning publicly traded securities and the accompanying securities' returns so that those actual security returns may more closely mirror the investors' expected returns. The long-term positive, constructive social change implication was that investors will lose less money and earn the expected returns for a more efficient capital market leading to a stronger economy and macroeconomic stability.

The preceding observation had meaning in a practical sense for investors worldwide with regard to the non-traditional, relative valuation and pricing of investment securities. If in the academic world professors would instruct their students, or if in the practitioner world securities brokers would instruct their clients, in the practices of relative pricing found in this study, the average investor would have a clear means for value determination to compare the various pricings of an investment security. The takeaway conclusion for this study was that with better comparisons of investment security relative pricing, investors could make better decisions concerning the avalanche of data available to consumers to make those decisions sensibly and build a better future for themselves, their families, and their nation.

References

Abdel-Jalil, T., & Thuniebat, A. (2009). Equity valuation in Amman Bourse. *Journal of Accounting, Business & Management, 16*(2), 15-27.

Aczel, A., & Sounderpandian, J. (2009). *Complete business statistics* (7th ed.). New York, NY: McGraw-Hill.

Afza, T., Slahudin, C., & Nazir, M. S. (2008). Diversification and corporate performance: An evaluation of Pakistani firms. *South Asian Journal of Management, 15*(3), 7-18.

Alkhalialeh, M. (2008). The relevancy of traditional performance measures in explaining stock returns variations in emerging economies: The case of Jordanian corporations. *The Business Review, Cambridge, 10*(1), 246-253.

American Psychological Association. (2011). Ethical principles of psychologists and code of conduct (2010 Amendments). Retrieved from http://www.apa.org/ethics/code/index.aspx

Ang, A., Goetzmann, W. N., & Schaefer, S. M. (2011). The efficient market theory and evidence: Implications for active investment management. *The Efficient Market Theory and Evidence* (pp. 170-196). Hanover, MA: Now Publishers, Inc.

Angrist, J., & Pischke, J. (2009). *Mostly harmless econometrics: An empiricist's companion.* Princeton, NJ: Princeton University Press.

Arends, B. (2010). The biggest lie about U.S. companies. *Marketwatch, The Wall Street Journal digital network, August 3, 2010.* Retrieved from http://www.marketwatch.com/story/the-biggest-lie-about-us-companies-2010-08-03

Armstrong, C. S., Davila, A., Foster, G., & Hand, J. R. M. (2011). Market-to-revenue multiples in public and private capital markets. *Australian Journal of Management, 36*(1), 15-57.

Balakrishnan, N. N., Davies, K. F., Keating, J. P., & Mason, R. L. (2011). Correlation-type goodness of fit test for extreme value distribution based on simultaneous closeness. *Communications In Statistics: Simulation & Computation, 40*(7), 1074-1095. doi:10.1080/03610918.2011.563004

Balog, J. (1975). Why the stock market reacts the way it does to announcements of mergers and acquisitions. *Financial Analysts Journal, 31*(2), 84-88.

Barbieri, A., Dubikovsky, V., Gladkevich, A., Goldberg, L. R., & Hayes, M. Y. (2010). Central limits and financial risk. *Quantitative Finance, 10*(10), 1091-1097. doi:10.1080/14697680903413597

Beaver, W. H., & Ryan, S. (2009). Risky debt, mixed-attribute accounting, and the identification of conditional conservatism. *Mixed-Attribute Accounting, and the Identification of Conditional Conservatism (September 23, 2009).*

Berkman, E. T., & Reise, S. P. (2012). *A conceptual guide to statistics using SPSS.* Thousand Oaks, CA: Sage Publications.

Bhalla, P. (2011). Determinants of mergers and acquisitions of firms in the Indian financial sector: An empirical analysis. *IUP Journal of Business Strategy, 8*(3), 7-23.

Bodie, Z., Kane, A., & Marcus, A. J. (2005). *Investments* (6th ed.). New York, NY: McGraw-Hill, Inc.

Boot, A. A., & Thakor, A. V. (2011). Managerial autonomy, allocation of control rights, and optimal capital structure. *Review Of Financial Studies, 24*(10), 3434-3485.

Bromiley, P. (2010). Looking at prospect theory. *Strategic Management Journal, 31*(12), 1357-1370.

Bryant, P., & Davis, C. (2012). Regulated change effects on boards of directors: A look at agency theory and resource dependency theory. *Academy of Strategic Management Journal, 11*(2), 1-15.

Campbell, R., & Selden, S. (2000). Does city-county consolidation save money? The unification of Athens-Clarke County suggests it might. *Public Policy Research Series, 1*(2), 1-2.

Chang, M. (2009). There is something about pairs trading. *Corporate Finance Review, 13*(5), 27-35.

Chen, N., Roll, R., & Ross, S. (1986). Economic forces and the stock market. *Journal of Business, 59*(3), 383–403.

Chou, P., Chou, R. K., & Ko, K. (2009). Prospect theory and the risk-return paradox: Some recent evidence. *Review of Quantitative Finance and Accounting, 33*(3), 193-208.

Clubb, C., & Naffi, M. (2007). The usefulness of book-to-market and ROE expectations for explaining UK stock returns. *Journal of Business Finance & Accounting, 34*(1-2), 1-32.

Committee on Science, Engineering, and Public Policy (U.S.), National Academy of Sciences (U.S.), National Academy of Engineering., & Institute of Medicine (U.S.). (2009). *On being a scientist: A guide to responsible conduct in research,* (3rd ed.). Washington, D.C: National Academies Press. Retrieved from the Committee on Science, Engineering, and Public Policy (U.S.), National Academy of Sciences (U.S.), National Academy of Engineering., & Institute of Medicine (U.S.) website: http://www.nap.edu/catalog.php?record_id=12192

Condie, S., & Ganguli, J. (2011). Informational efficiency with ambiguous information. *Economic Theory, 48*(2/3), 229-242. doi:10.1007/s00199-011-0646-2

Creswell, J. (2009). *Research design: Qualitative, quantitative, and mixed methods approaches* (3rd ed.). Thousand Oaks, CA: Sage Publications.

Dammon, R. M., & Senbet, L. W. (2012). The effect of taxes and depreciation on corporate investment and financial leverage. *The Journal of Finance, 43*(2), 357-373.

Damodaran, A. (2007). Return on capital (ROC), return on invested capital (ROIC) and return on equity (ROE): Measurement and implications. *The Stern School of Business, New York University.* Retrieved from http://pages.stern.nyu.edu/~adamodar/

Damodaran, A. (2006). Valuation approaches and metrics: A survey of the theory and evidence. *The Stern School of Business, New York University.* Retrieved from http://pages.stern.nyu.edu/~adamodar/

Donelson, D. C., Jennings, R., & McInnis, J. (2011). Changes over time in the revenue-expense relation: Accounting or economics?. *Accounting Review, 86*(3), 945-974. doi:10.2308/accr.00000046

Duran, R., Eisenhart, M., Erickson, F., Grant, C., Green, J., Hedges, L., Levine, F., Moss, P., Pellegrino, J., & Schneider, B. (2006). Standards for reporting on empirical social science research in AERA publications. *Educational Researcher, 35*(6), 33–40.

Editorial. (2011, May 6). NYSE daily volume statistics: Who is trading? *The New York*

Times, paras. 1-8. Retrieved from http://statspotting.com/nyse-daily-volume-statistics-who-is-trading/ on February 26, 2013.

Eiteman, D., Stonehill, A., & Moffett, M. (2007). *Multinational business finance* (11th ed.). Boston, MA: Pearson: Addison-Wesley.

Elton, E. J., Gruber, M. J., & Blake, C. R. (2011). Holdings data, security returns, and the selection of superior mutual funds. *Journal Of Financial & Quantitative Analysis, 46*(2), 341-367. doi:10.1017/S0022109011000019

Fama, E. F., & French, K. R. (2004). The capital asset pricing model: Theory and evidence. *Journal Of Economic Perspectives, 18*(3), 25-46.

Fernandez, P. (2007). A more realistic valuation: Adjusted present value and WACC with constant book leverage ratio. *Journal of Applied Finance, 17*(2), 13-20.

Garvey, J. (2010). An investigation into risk propensity in bull and bear markets. *Journal of Risk Research, 13*(6), 789-804. doi:10.1080/13669870903560283

Gentry, R., & Shen, W. (2010). The relationship between accounting and market measures of firm financial performance: How strong is it? *Journal of Managerial Issues, 22*(4), 514-530.

Gilliam, J., Chatterjee, S., & Grable, J. (2010). Measuring the perception of financial risk tolerance: A tale of two measures. *Journal Of Financial Counseling & Planning, 21*(2), 30-43.

Gomes, M., Henriques-Rodrigues, L., & Miranda, M. (2011). Reduced-Bias Location-Invariant Extreme Value Index Estimation: A Simulation Study. *Communications In Statistics: Simulation & Computation, 40*(3), 424-447. doi:10.1080/03610918.2010.543297

Grauer, R. (2008). On the predictability of stock market returns: Evidence from industry-rotation strategies. *Journal of Business and Management, 14*(2), 149-173.

Grinold, R. (2011). The Description of Portfolios. *Journal Of Portfolio Management, 37*(2), 15-30.

Gubler, Z. (2011). The financial innovation process: Theory and application. *Delaware Journal of Corporate Law, 36*(1), 55-119.

Guillot, P., & Fung, S. (2010). Pharmaceutical medical information contact centers:

Results of three benchmarking surveys. *Drug Information Journal, 44*(5), 569-579.

Guni, C. N., & Negurita, O. (2011). Accounting standards and financial reports, guilty for the actual crisis? *Economics, Management and Financial Markets, 6*(1), 975-981.

Hackmann, R., Yi, X., & Valeva, A. (2010). The real U.S. role and position in the world economy. *International Journal of Business and Management, 5*(11), 15-25.

Haymore, S. J. (2011). Public(ly oriented) companies: B corporations and the Delaware stakeholder provision dilemma. *Vanderbilt Law Review, 64*(4), 1311-1346.

Heintz, J., & Parry, R. (2008). *College accounting* (19th ed.). Mason, OH: South-Western, Thomson Learning.

Hobbs, J., & Sharma, V. (2011). A survey data response to the teaching of utility curves and risk aversion. *Journal Of Education For Business, 86*(2), 59-63. doi:10.1080/08832321003774780

Hodnett, K., & Heng-Hsing, H. (2012). Capital market theories: Market efficiency versus investor prospects. *International Business & Economics Research Journal, 11*(8), 849-862.

Horner, J., & Minifie, F. D. (2011). Research ethics I: Responsible conduct of research (RCR)-historical and contemporary issues pertaining to human and animal experimentation. *Journal of Speech, Language and Hearing Research, 54*(1), 303-329.

Jalbert, T., Briley, J. E., & Jalbert, M. (2012). Forecasting financial statements using risk management associates industry data. *Business Education & Accreditation, 4*(1), 123-134.

Johnstone, D. (2007). The value of a probability forecast from portfolio theory. *Theory and Decision, 63*(2), 153-203.

Kanji, G. K. (2006). *100 statistical tests* (3rd ed.). Thousand Oaks, CA: Sage Publications.

Khan, M. I. (2012). Non-standardized form of CAPM and stock returns. *International Journal of Business and Social Science, 3*(2), 193-201.

Kim, D., & Qi, Y. (2010). Accruals quality, stock returns, and macroeconomic conditions. *Accounting Review*, *85*(3), 937-978.

Kopelman, R. E. (2010). Validity evidence for the cube one framework: Examination of objective data. *Journal of Global Business Management, 6*(1), 1-7.

Lan, L., & Heracleous, L. (2010). Rethinking agency theory: The view from law. *Academy Of Management Review*, *35*(2), 294-314. doi:10.5465/AMR.2010.48463335

Lee, C., Ng, D., & Swaminathan, B. (2009). Testing international asset pricing models using implied costs of capital. *Journal of Financial & Quantitative Analysis*, *44*(2), 307-335.

Lintner, J. (1965a). The valuation of risk assets and the selection of risky investments in stock portfolios and capital budgets. *Review of Economics and Statistics, 47*(1), 13-37.

Lintner, J. (1965b). Security prices, risk, and maximal gains from diversification. *The Journal of Finance 20*(4), 587-615.

Mangram, M. E. (2013). A simplified perspective of the Markowitz portfolio theory. *Global Journal Of Business Research (GJBR)*, *7*(1), 59-70.

Markowitz, H. (1952a). Portfolio selection. *The Journal of Finance 7*(1), 77-91.

Markowitz, H. (1952b). The utility of wealth. *The Journal of Political Economy, 60*(2), 151–158.

Markowitz, H. (1959). *Portfolio selection*. BookCrafters, Inc: Chelsea, MI.

Mcdonald, J. B., Michelfelder, R. A., & Theodossiou, P. (2010). Robust estimation with flexible parametric distributions: estimation of utility stock betas. *Quantitative Finance*, *10*(4), 375-387. doi:10.1080/14697680902814241

McGowan, G. (2011). Guide to investor-owned utilities: Private utilities serve the public sector. In *Business.com*. Retrieved from http://www.business.com/guides/investor-owned-utilities-11916/

McNerney, R. (2007). Electric power industry overview 2007. *Independent Statistics & Analysis, U.S. Energy Information Administration (EIA), The U.S. Department of Energy (DOE)*. Retrieved from http://eia.gov/cneaf/electricity/page/prim2/toc2.html

Mirza, N., & Afzal, A. (2011). Size and value premium in international portfolios: Evidence from 15 European countries. *Finance a Uver,-Czech Journal of Economics and Finance, 61*(2), 173-190.

Modigliani, F., & Miller, M. (1958). The cost of capital, corporation finance and the theory of investment. *American Economic Review, 48*(3), 261-297.

Mondher, K. (2011). A re-examination of the MM capital structure irrelevance theorem: A partial payout approach. *International Journal of Business and Management, 6*(10), 193-204.

Morelli, D. (2012). Security returns, beta, size, and book-to-market equity: Evidence from the Shanghai A-share market. *Review Of Quantitative Finance & Accounting, 38*(1), 47-60. doi:10.1007/s11156-010-0218-8

Morrison, M., & Brown, T. C. (2009).Testing the effectiveness of certainty scales, cheap talk, and dissonance-minimization in reducing hypothetical bias in contingent valuation studies. *Environmental and Resource Economics, 44*(3), 307-326.

Mossin, J. (1966). Equilibrium in a capital asset market. *Econometrica, 34*(4), 768-783.

Muiño, F., & Trombetta, M. (2009). Does graph disclosure bias reduce the cost of equity capital? *Accounting and Business Research, 39*(2), 83-102.

Mukherji, S., & Youngho, L. (2013). Explanatory factors for market multiples and expected returns. *International Journal Of Business & Finance Research (IJBFR), 7*(1), 45-54.

Newton, R. R., & Rudestam, K. E. (1999). *Your statistical consultant: Answers to your data analysis questions.* Thousand Oaks, CA: Sage Publications.

Olivero, M. (2010). Government spending, distortionary taxation and the international transmission of business cycles. *Journal of Economic Integration, 25*(2), 403-426.

Ozel, N. B. (2010). *Earnings and cash flows in debt evaluation by private debt holders.* (Columbia University). *ProQuest Dissertations and Theses,* Retrieved from http://search.proquest.com/docview/853645250?accountid=28180

Pan, H. (2011). A basic theory of intelligent finance. *New Mathematics & Natural Computation, 7*(2), 197-227.

Pfau, W. D. (2012). Capital market expectations, asset allocation, and safe withdrawal rates. *Journal Of Financial Planning, 25*(1), 36-43.

Prado-Lorenzo, J., Rodriguez-Dominguez, L., Gallego-Alvarez, I., & Garcia-Sanchez, I. (2009). Factors influencing the disclosure of greenhouse gas emissions in companies world-wide. *Management Decision, 47*(7), 1133-1157.

Rachdi, H., & Ameur, I. (2011). Board characteristics, performance and risk taking behaviour in Tunisian banks. *International Journal of Business and Management, 6*(6), 88-97.

Riedl, E. J. (2002). *An examination of long-lived asset impairments.* The Pennsylvania State University). *ProQuest Dissertations and Theses*, 61-61 p. Retrieved from http://search.proquest.com/docview/305486530?accountid=14872.

Roll, R., & Ross, S. A. (1980). An empirical investigation of the arbitrage pricing theory. *The Journal of Finance, 35*(5), 1073-1103.

Rondinelli, D. A., & Burpitt, W. J. (2000). Do government incentives attract and retain international investment? A study of foreign-owned firms in North Carolina. *Policy Sciences, 33*(2), 181-205.

Ross, S. (1976). The arbitrage theory of capital asset pricing. *Journal of Economic Theory, 13*(1976), 341-360.

Samuelson, P., & Nordhaus, W. (1995). *Economics.* New York: McGraw-Hill, Inc.

Sehgal, S., & Pandey, A. (2010). Equity valuation using price multiples: A comparative study for BRICKS. *Asian Journal of Finance & Accounting, 2*(1), 68-91.

Shapiro, D. L. (1970). Conglomerate Mergers and Optimal Investment Policy. *Journal Of Financial & Quantitative Analysis, 4*(5), 643-656. doi:10.2307/2330118

Sharpe, W. (1964). Capital asset prices: A theory of market equilibrium under conditions of risk. *The Journal of Finance, 19*(3), 425-442.

Sharpe, W. (1965). Risk-aversion in the stock market: Some empirical evidence. *The Journal of Finance, 20*(3), 416-422.

Shelor, R., & Wright, S. (2011). A teaching tool for computing stock returns, risk and beta. *Business Education & Accreditation, 3*(1), 1-7.

Shim, J., Siegel, J., & Lansner, J. (1994). *100 investment decision tools.* Chicago, IL: International Publishing Corporation.

Stickney, C., & Weil, R. (2003). *Financial accounting* (10th ed.). Mason, OH: South-Western, Thomson Learning.

Treynor, J. (1962). *Toward a theory of market value of risky assets.* Unpublished manuscript. Available at SSRN: http://ssrn.com/abstract=628187 or http://dx.doi.org/10.2139/ssrn.628187

Turnbull, S. (2009). Measuring and managing risk in innovative financial instruments. *The Journal of Credit Risk, 5*(2), 87-114.

Umutlu, M. (2010). Firm leverage and investment decisions in an emerging market. *Quality & Quantity, 44*(5), 1005-1013. doi:10.1007/s11135-009-9250-y

Wang, J. (2008). Investigating market value and intellectual capital for S&P 500. *Journal of Intellectual Capital, 9*(4), 546-563.

Wang, Y., Chen, S., & Cheng, Y. (2011). Revisiting corporate dividends and seasoned equity issues. *Review Of Quantitative Finance & Accounting, 36*(1), 133-151. doi:10.1007/s11156-010-0221-0

Wei, H., Qianqiu, L., Rhee, S., & Liang, Z. (2010). Return reversals, idiosyncratic risk, and expected returns. *Review Of Financial Studies, 23*(1), 147-168. doi:10.1093/rfs/hhp015

Xian, C., Chen, H., & Moldousupova, A. (2011). Investment, earnings management and equity-based compensation. *Journal Of Accounting, Business & Management, 18*(2), 121-136.

Yockey, R. D. (2011). *SPSS demystified: A step-by-step guide to successful data analysis* (2nd ed.). Upper Saddle River, NJ: Pearson Education, Inc.

You, H., & Zhang, X. (2009). Financial reporting complexity and investor underreaction to 10-K information. *Review of Accounting Studies, 14*(4), 559-586.

Zakamulin, V. (2011). Sharpe (ratio) thinking about the investment opportunity set and CAPM relationship. *Economics Research International, 2011*, 1-9. doi:10.1155/2011/781760

Appendix A: Firm Market Capitalization Categorical Classifications

Large-cap classification formula: Large-cap   = Shares times Price

Medium-cap classification formula: Medium-cap = Shares times Price

Small-cap classification formula: Small-cap   = Shares times Price

Legend

Shares   = The number of outstanding shares of the company's securities (diluted, to account for the types of securities convertible to common stock–e.g. convertible bonds).

Price   = The amount of U.S. dollars and cents per outstanding share of the security (in this particular case, shares of common stock).

Large-cap   = Market capitalization that equals $5 billion U.S. dollars or more.

Medium-cap = Market capitalization of more than $1 billion U.S., but less than $5 billion U.S. dollars.

Small-cap   = Market capitalization that equals $1 billion U.S. dollars or less.

Appendix B: Population for the Study

The Listing of the 160 Publicly Traded Electric Utility Companies

1)   Alabama Power - [Southern Company]

2)   Allegheny Power [east coast holding company]

3)   Alliant - Formed by the merger of three strong energy-services providers.

4)   Alpena Power Company

5)   American Electric Power - (featuring interactive industrial site database)

6)   Ameren - (Union Electric & CIPSCO)

7)   APS - Arizona

8)   Atlantic Energy east coast [Delmarva Power & Atlantic Energy]

9)   Avista Corporation

10)   Baltimore Gas and Electric – Maryland

11)   Bangor Hydro - Maine

12)   Bear Valley Electric Service - California

13)   Black Hills Corporation - in the Dakotas

14)   Boston Edison – Massachusetts

15)   Carolina Power & Light Company

16)   Central and Southwest System - CP&L~PSO~SWEPCo~WTU

17)   Central Hudson Gas & Electric Corporation - New York

18)   Central Illinois Light Company

19)   Central Maine Power Company

20)   Central Vermont Public Service Corp.

21)   Citizens' Electric Company

22)   Citizens Utilities nation wide

23)   CLECO - Louisiana

24)   CMP Group - [holding company]

25)   CMS Energy - Michigan

26)   Commonwealth Energy

27)   COM/Electric - Massachusetts

28)   Con Edison - Consolidated Edison, New York

29)   Conectiv [Delmarva Power & Atlantic Energy]

30)   Connecticut Light & Power Company

31)   Consumers Energy Company - Michigan

32)   CONVEX - Connecticut Valley Electric Exchange

33)   Dayton Power & Light Co. Ohio

34)   Delmarva Power & Light - [Delmarva Power & Atlantic Energy]

35)   Detroit Edison - Michigan

36)   Dominion Resources

37)   DQE - [Duquesne Light Company] - Pennsylvania

38)   DTE Energy

39)   Duke Energy Carolinas, LLC

40)   Duke Energy Indiana, Inc.

41)   Duke Energy Ohio, Inc.

42)   Duke Energy Kentucky, Inc.

43)   Eastern Utilities - Massachusetts

44)   Edison International - southern California

45)   Edison Sault Electric Company - Michigan

46)   El Paso Electric Company - Texas

47)   Empire District Electric Company - Missouri

48)   Energy West

49)   Entergy Corporation - south central US & international

50)   FirstEnergy - Holding company

51)   Florida Power & Light Company

52)   Florida Progress Corporation

53)   Florida Power Corporation

54)   Florida Public Utilities Company

55)   General Public Utilities System - eastern US

56)   Georgia Power - [Southern Company]

57)   Granite State Electric

58)   Green Mountain Power Corporation- Vermont

59)   Gulf Power Company - [Southern Company]

60)   Hawaiian Electric Company

61)   Hawaiian Electric Industries

62)	Houston Industries

63)	Houston Lighting & Power Company – Texas

64)	IDACORP - (holding company)

65)	Idaho Power Company

66)	IES Industries [Alliant]

67)	Illinois Power

68)	Illinova

69)	Indianapolis Power & Light Company - [IPALCO]

70)	Interstate Power Company

71)	Island Energy – California

72)	Kansas City Power & Light Company

73)	Kauai Electric

74)	KU Energy Corporation – Kentucky

75)	LG&E Energy - Kentucky

76)	Lockhart Power Company - South Carolina

77)	Madison Gas and Electric - Wisconsin

78)	Maine Public Service Company

79)	Massachusetts Electric Company

80)	MidAmerican Energy - Illinois, Iowa, South Dakota

81)	Minnesota Power

82)	Mississippi Power Company - [Southern Company]

83)   Modern Electric Water Company - Washington.

84)   Montana Power Company

85)   Montana-Dakota Utilities Co.

86)   Nantahala Power and Light

87)   Narragansett Electric - [NEES]

88)   National Grid USA

89)   NEES - New England Electric System

90)   Nevada Power Company

91)   New Century Energies (formerly PSC CO & SWPSC)

92)   New Jersey Resources Corporation

93)   New York State Electric & Gas

94)   Newport Electric

95)   Niagara Mohawk - New York

96)   Northeast Utilities

97)   Northern Indiana Public Service Company

98)   Northern States Power

99)   Northwestern Public Service - South Dakota

100)   NSTAR

101)   Ohio Edison

102)   Oklahoma Gas & Electric

103)   Orange & Rockland Utilities - New York, Pennsylvania

104)   Otter Tail Power Company- north central US

105)   Pacific Enterprises - holding company

106)   Pacific Gas & Electric

107)   PacifiCorp - [Pacific Power, Utah Power]

108)   PECO Energy – Pennsylvania

109)   Pennsylvania Power Company

110)   Peoples Energy Corporation - holding company

111)   Pinnacle West

112)   PNM - New Mexico

113)   Portland General Electric Co.

114)   Potomac Electric Power Company

115)   PP&L, Inc.

116)   PP&L Resources - Central Eastern Pennsylvania

117)   Public Service Company of New Mexico

118)   Public Service Electric and Gas - New Jersey

119)   Public Service Enterprise Group - New Jersey

120)   Public Service of New Hampshire

121)   Rochester Gas & Electric - New York

122)   San Diego Gas & Electric - [Enova]

123)   Savannah Electric

124)   SCANA Corporation - SCE&G

125)   Sempra Energy [holding company]

126)   Sierra Pacific - Nevada & California

127)   Southern California Edison - [Edison International]

128)   The Southern Company - Alabama Power ~ Georgia Power ~ Gulf Power

129)   Southern Indiana Gas and Electric Company

130)   STP Nuclear Operating Company - Texas.

131)   St. Joseph Light & Power – Missouri

132)   Tampa Electric – Florida

133)   TECO Energy – Florida

134)   Tennessee Power Company

135)   Texas Utilities System - holding company

136)   Texas-New Mexico Power Company

137)   TNP Enterprises, Inc. Texas, New Mexico

138)   Tucson Electric Power

139)   TXU

140)   TXU Electric & Gas

141)   UGI Corporation - Pennsylvania gas and electric utility & propane

142)   Union Electric – AmerenUE

143)   Unicom Corporation - [Commonwealth Edison]

144)   UI - United Illuminating Company

145)   UniSource Energy Corporation

146)   UNITIL - US northeast

147)   Upper Peninsula Power Company

148)   UtiliCorp United - Energy One

149)   Virginia Power

150)   Wellsboro Electric Company

151)   Western Massachusetts Electric Company

152)   Western Resources - KPL ~ KG&E

153)   Wisconsin Electric

154)   Wisconsin Energy Corporation

155)   Wisconsin Fuel and Light Company

156)   Wisconsin Power and Light Co.

157)   Wisconsin Public Service Corporation

158)   WPS Resources Corporation - holding company

159)   Xcel Energy

160)   Yankee Atomic Electric Company

Listing of the Investor Owned Electric Utility Companies. Retrieved from

http://www.utilityconnection.com/page2b.asp

Appendix C: Statistical Power Calculations for the Study

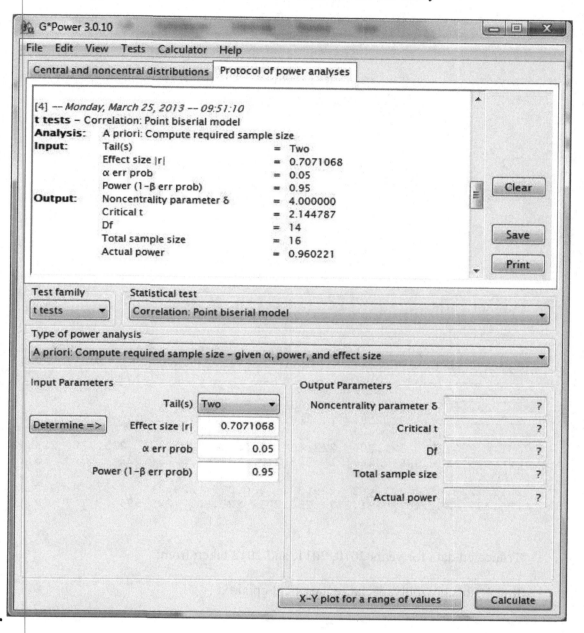

Appendix D: Consumer Price Index Data

U.S. Department Of Labor

Bureau of Labor Statistics

Washington, D.C. 20212

Consumer Price Index

All Urban Consumers - (CPI-U)

U.S. city average

All items

1982-84=100

Percent change

```
Annual    Dec-   Avg-
     Year  Jan.       Feb.      Mar.      Apr.      May       June      July
Aug.      Sep.      Oct.      Nov.      Dec.      Avg.      Dec       Avg


2010  216.687  216.741  217.631  218.009  218.178  217.965  218.011
218.312  218.439  218.711  218.803  219.179  218.056    1.5    1.6

2011  220.223  221.309  223.467  224.906  225.964  225.722  225.922
226.545  226.889  226.421  226.230  225.672  224.939    3.0    3.2

2012  226.665  227.663  229.392  230.085  229.815  229.478  229.104
230.379  231.407  231.317  230.221  229.601  229.594    1.7    2.1
```

Truncated data for years 2010, 2011, and 2012 taken from:

ftp://ftp.bls.gov/pub/special.requests/cpi/cpiai.txt

Appendix E: Sample Firm Market Prices and Associated Data

CIK	*Beta*	MP1 2010	MP1 2011	MP1 2012	MP1 AVG.
2224	0.49	$26.32	$29.42	$28.63	$28.12
6160	0.61	$53.43	$66.00	$63.80	$61.08
3068	0.95	$19.39	$21.78	$20.31	$20.49
0464	1.3	$30.00	$33.58	$36.34	$33.31
1728	1.2	$42.76	$46.77	$50.95	$46.83
1138	0.88	$35.84	$36.92	$42.42	$38.39
3308	0.66	$51.99	$60.88	$69.19	$60.69
2910	0.92	$28.19	$33.13	$30.72	$30.68
3088	0.93	$28.83	$35.79	$34.73	$33.12
2541	0.86	$36.77	$44.11	$43.91	$41.60
9819	0.92	$30.76	$38.10	$40.01	$36.29
2208	0.85	$52.48	$55.00	$70.94	$59.47
2903	0.65	$23.55	$27.64	$26.71	$25.97
7877	1.1	$36.98	$42.41	$43.35	$40.91
6863	1.03	$48.51	$54.18	$52.22	$51.64
7052	0.49	$38.60	$41.40	$45.19	$41.73

Appendix F: Sample Firm Book Prices

CIK	BV2 2010	BV2 2011	BV2 2012	BV2 AVG.
2224	$16.98	$18.72	$18.01	$17.90
6160	$16.59	$16.78	$30.11	$30.32
3068	$21.56	$22.02	$22.01	$21.86
0464	$28.02	$27.55	$27.84	$27.80
1728	$22.72	$23.84	$25.07	$23.87
1138	$22.69	$23.41	$25.74	$23.95
3308	$34.35	$35.90	$37.91	$36.05
2910	$32.30	$32.75	$27.20	$30.75
3088	$22.64	$23.67	$25.08	$23.80
2541	$28.30	$28.99	$30.09	$29.13
9819	$19.24	$21.15	$22.84	$21.08
2208	$36.39	$39.18	$40.88	$38.82
2903	$16.96	$17.42	$18.17	$17.52
7877	$31.00	$33.19	$35.07	$33.09
6863	$37.91	$38.48	$39.24	$38.54
7052	$32.48	$30.86	$28.95	$30.76

Appendix G: Sample Firm Return-on-Assets

CIK	ROA3 2010	ROA3 2011	ROA3 2012	ROA3 AVG.
2224	3.52%	3.53%	2.80%	3.28%
6160	2.23%	2.73%	1.55%	2.17%
3068	2.38%	1.90%	2.06%	2.11%
0464	1.85%	1.20%	2.19%	1.75%
1728	4.38%	4.18%	4.06%	4.21%
1138	2.98%	2.76%	2.20%	2.64%
3308	3.69%	3.36%	2.97%	3.34%
2910	3.52%	2.19%	2.80%	3.28%
3088	2.55%	2.88%	2.82%	2.75%
2541	3.10%	3.13%	2.97%	3.07%
9819	3.52%	4.83%	3.95%	3.28%
2208	2.34%	4.00%	2.35%	2.90%
2903	2.74%	2.83%	2.91%	2.83%
7877	3.05%	3.36%	3.17%	3.20%
6863	2.25%	2.28%	2.72%	2.42%
7052	2.76%	3.53%	2.80%	0.76%

Appendix H: Sample Firm Market Value-to-Book Value

CIK	NTRFP4 2010	NTRFP4 2011	NTRFP4 2012	NTRFP4 AVG.
2224	1.55	1.57	1.59	1.57
6160	3.22	3.93	2.12	3.09
3068	0.9	0.99	0.92	0.94
0464	1.07	1.22	1.31	1.2
1728	1.88	1.96	2.03	1.96
1138	1.58	1.58	1.65	1.6
3308	1.51	1.7	1.83	1.68
2910	0.87	1.01	1.13	1
3088	1.27	1.51	1.38	1.39
2541	1.3	1.52	1.46	1.43
9819	1.6	1.8	1.75	1.72
2208	1.44	1.4	1.74	1.53
2903	1.39	1.59	1.47	1.48
7877	1.19	1.28	1.24	1.24
6863	1.28	1.41	1.33	1.34
7052	1.19	1.34	1.56	1.36

Appendix I: Sample Firm Variant Prices

CIK	CMVCP5 2010	CMVCP5 2011	CMVCP5 2012	CMVCP5 AVG.
2224	-8.5	-0.12	-7.9	-5.51
6160	-10.7	-0.3	-9.98	-6.99
3068	-16.61	-0.47	-15.51	-10.86
0464	-22.7	-0.64	-21.22	-14.85
1728	-20.93	-0.56	-19.57	-13.69
1138	-15.38	-0.43	-14.37	-10.06
3308	-11.55	-0.32	-10.78	-7.55
2910	-16.1	-0.45	-15.09	-10.55
3088	-16.26	-0.45	-15.18	-10.63
2541	-15.03	-0.41	-14.04	-9.83
9819	-16.05	-0.42	-15.01	-10.49
2208	-14.87	-0.4	-13.88	-9.72
2903	-11.39	-0.32	-10.62	-7.44
7877	-19.21	-0.52	-17.95	-12.56
6863	-18	-0.5	-16.81	-11.77
7052	-8.6	-0.27	-8.05	-5.64

Appendix J: Sample Firm Market Capitalization

CIK	CMC6_2010	CMC6_2011	CMC6_2012	CMC6_AVG.	CMC6 AVG cat.
2224	$12,722,851,120	$17,016,675,100	$16,661,056,720	$15,466,860,980	large
6160	$71,016,179,468	$88,164,859,926	$44,956,914,099	$68,045,984,498	large
3068	$2,631,034,452	$2,965,587,974	$3,118,657,327	$2,905,093,251	medium
0464	$1,177,863,540	$1,475,144,954	$1,607,060,295	$1,420,022,930	medium
1728	$988,339,161	$1,081,024,849	$1,177,639,856	$1,082,334,622	medium
1138	$1,311,950,008	$1,401,341,759	$1,755,614,015	$1,489,635,261	medium
3308	$21,885,314,028	$25,338,789,370	$29,327,379,041	$25,517,160,813	large
2910	$6,741,116,647	$8,003,761,871	$7,453,737,093	$7,399,538,537	large
3088	$1,044,575,162	$1,299,126,500	$1,293,433,657	$1,212,378,440	medium
2541	$4,077,101,320	$4,896,591,596	$4,873,611,473	$4,615,768,129	medium
9819	$1,874,814,802	$2,317,455,512	$2,414,871,927	$2,202,380,747	medium
2208	$12,621,721,030	$13,232,486,960	$17,259,049,707	$14,371,085,899	large
2903	$11,367,269,501	$13,455,939,768	$13,042,066,174	$12,621,758,481	large
7877	$1,827,750,700	$2,118,256,426	$2,173,717,084	$2,039,908,070	medium
6863	$3,784,162,501	$4,241,638,747	$4,094,052,595	$4,039,951,281	medium
7052	$12,576,312,552	$13,488,583,928	$14,723,408,399	$13,596,101,626	large

Appendix K: Critical Values for the *w/s* Normality Test

100 STATISTICAL TESTS

Table 14 Critical values of w/s for the normality test

Columns *a* denote the lower boundaries or the left-sided critical values.
Columns *b* denote the upper boundaries or the right-sided critical values.

	Level of significance α											
	0.000		0.005		0.01		0.025		0.05		0.10	
n	a	b	a	b	a	b	a	b	a	b	a	b
3	1.732	2.000	1.735	2.000	1.737	2.000	1.745	2.000	1.758	1.999	1.782	1.997
4	1.732	2.449	1.82	2.447	1.87	2.445	1.93	2.439	1.98	2.429	2.04	2.409
5	1.826	2.828	1.98	2.813	2.02	2.803	2.09	2.782	2.15	2.753	2.22	2.712
6	1.826	3.162	2.11	3.115	2.15	3.095	2.22	3.056	2.28	3.012	2.37	2.949
7	1.871	3.464	2.22	3.369	2.26	3.338	2.33	3.282	2.40	3.222	2.49	3.143
8	1.871	3.742	2.31	3.585	2.35	3.543	2.43	3.471	2.50	3.399	2.59	3.308
9	1.897	4.000	2.39	3.772	2.44	3.720	2.51	3.634	2.59	3.552	2.68	3.449
10	1.897	4.243	2.46	3.935	2.51	3.875	2.59	3.777	2.67	3.685	2.76	3.57
11	1.915	4.472	2.53	4.079	2.58	4.012	2.66	3.903	2.74	3.80	2.84	3.68
12	1.915	4.690	2.59	4.208	2.64	4.134	2.72	4.02	2.80	3.91	2.90	3.78
13	1.927	4.899	2.64	4.325	2.70	4.244	2.78	4.12	2.86	4.00	2.96	3.87
14	1.927	5.099	2.70	4.431	2.75	4.34	2.83	4.21	2.92	4.09	3.02	3.95
15	1.936	5.292	2.74	4.53	2.80	4.44	2.88	4.29	2.97	4.17	3.07	4.02
16	1.936	5.477	2.79	4.62	2.84	4.52	2.93	4.37	3.01	4.24	3.12	4.09
17	1.944	5.657	2.83	4.70	2.88	4.60	2.97	4.44	3.06	4.31	3.17	4.15
18	1.944	5.831	2.87	4.78	2.92	4.67	3.01	4.51	3.10	4.37	3.21	4.21
19	1.949	6.000	2.90	4.85	2.96	4.74	3.05	4.56	3.14	4.43	3.25	4.27
20	1.949	6.164	2.94	4.91	2.99	4.80	3.09	4.63	3.18	4.49	3.29	4.32
25	1.961	6.93	3.09	5.19	3.15	5.06	3.24	4.87	3.34	4.71	3.45	4.53
30	1.966	7.62	3.21	5.40	3.27	5.26	3.37	5.06	3.47	4.89	3.59	4.70
35	1.972	8.25	3.32	5.57	3.38	5.42	3.48	5.21	3.58	5.04	3.70	4.84
40	1.975	8.83	3.41	5.71	3.47	5.56	3.57	5.34	3.67	5.16	3.79	4.96
45	1.978	9.38	3.49	5.83	3.55	5.67	3.66	5.45	3.75	5.26	3.88	5.06
50	1.980	9.90	3.56	5.93	3.62	5.77	3.73	5.54	3.83	5.35	3.95	5.14
55	1.982	10.39	3.62	6.02	3.69	5.86	3.80	5.63	3.90	5.43	4.02	5.22
60	1.983	10.86	3.68	6.10	3.75	5.94	3.86	5.70	3.96	5.51	4.08	5.29
65	1.985	11.31	3.74	6.17	3.80	6.01	3.91	5.77	4.01	5.57	4.14	5.35
70	1.986	11.75	3.79	6.24	3.85	6.07	3.96	5.83	4.06	5.63	4.19	5.41
75	1.987	12.17	3.83	6.30	3.90	6.13	4.01	5.88	4.11	5.68	4.24	5.46
80	1.987	12.57	3.88	6.35	3.94	6.18	4.05	5.93	4.16	5.73	4.28	5.51
85	1.988	12.96	3.92	6.40	3.99	6.23	4.09	5.98	4.20	5.78	4.33	5.56
90	1.989	13.34	3.96	6.45	4.02	6.27	4.13	6.03	4.24	5.82	4.36	5.60
95	1.990	13.71	3.99	6.49	4.06	6.32	4.17	6.07	4.27	5.86	4.40	5.64
100	1.990	14.07	4.03	6.53	4.10	6.36	4.21	6.11	4.31	5.90	4.44	5.68
150	1.993	17.26	4.32	6.82	4.38	6.64	4.48	6.39	4.59	6.18	4.72	5.96
200	1.995	19.95	4.53	7.01	4.59	6.84	4.68	6.60	4.78	6.39	4.90	6.15
500	1.998	31.59	5.06	7.60	5.13	7.42	5.25	7.15	5.47	6.94	5.49	6.72
1000	1.999	44.70	5.50	7.99	5.57	7.80	5.68	7.54	5.79	7.33	5.92	7.11

Taken from Kanji, G. K. (2006). *100 statistical tests* (3rd ed.). Thousand Oaks, CA: Sage Publications, p. 210.

Appendix L: Sample Firm Study-Adjusted Prices and Values

CIK	MP1_2012	Adj_BV2_2012	ROA3 2012	Adj_NTRFP4_2012	Amt_Deriv_needed
2224	$28.63	$55.30	2.80%	0.52	$22,674,000,000
6160	$63.80	$102.93	1.55%	0.62	$31,944,000,000
3068	$20.31	$40.82	2.06%	0.5	$2,889,300,000
0464	$36.34	$56.38	2.19%	0.64	$1,264,453,000
1728	$50.95	$43.59	4.06%	1.17	$428,066,000
1138	$42.42	$74.30	2.20%	0.57	$2,009,499,000
3308	$69.19	$114.12	2.97%	0.61	$32,303,000,000
2910	$30.72	$62.66	2.80%	0.49	$8,603,000,000
3088	$34.73	$68.51	2.82%	0.51	$1,617,469,000
2541	$43.91	$67.08	2.97%	0.65	$4,105,500,000
9819	$40.01	$41.88	3.95%	0.96	$1,148,923,000
2208	$70.94	$105.56	2.35%	0.67	$15,737,000,000
2903	$26.71	$45.60	2.91%	0.59	$13,392,532,000
7877	$43.35	$71.01	3.17%	0.61	$1,802,010,000
6863	$52.22	$92.48	2.72%	0.56	$4,173,800,000
7052	$45.19	$107.31	2.80%	0.42	$25,530,000,000

Appendix M: Sample Firm Hypothesis 3 Dataset 1

Sample of 16 coded sample firms (H0: 3 data set for analysis)

CIK	2012_Debt_Ratio	MP1_AVG	BV2_AVG	NTRFP4_AVG
2224	75.98%	$28.12	$17.90	1.57
6160	64.03%	$61.08	$30.32	2.75
3068	64.97%	$20.49	$21.86	0.94
0464	66.95%	$33.31	$27.80	1.20
1728	63.49%	$46.83	$23.87	1.96
1138	74.27%	$38.39	$23.95	1.60
3308	75.06%	$60.69	$36.05	1.68
2910	69.70%	$30.68	$30.75	1.00
3088	73.20%	$33.12	$23.80	1.39
2541	69.03%	$41.60	$29.13	1.43
9819	63.85%	$36.29	$21.08	1.72
2208	71.56%	$59.47	$38.82	1.53
2903	71.50%	$25.97	$17.52	1.48
7877	66.94%	$40.91	$33.09	1.24
6863	70.21%	$51.64	$38.54	1.34
7052	78.75%	$41.73	$30.76	1.36

Appendix N: Sample Firm Hypothesis 3 Dataset 2

Sample of 16 coded sample firms (H0: 3 stage two regression analysis data)

CIK	2012_debt	2012_assets	2012_debt_ratio	MP1_AVG	BV2_AVG	NTRFP4_AVG
2224	$33,154,000,000	$43,634,000,000	75.98%	$28.12	$17.90	1.57
6160	$72,900,000,000	$113,856,000,000	64.03%	$61.08	$30.32	2.75
3068	$6,268,300,000	$9,647,300,000	64.97%	$20.49	$21.86	0.94
0464	$2,496,962,000	$3,729,471,000	66.95%	$33.31	$27.80	1.2
1728	$1,007,495,000	$1,586,924,000	63.49%	$46.83	$23.87	1.96
1138	$3,074,964,000	$4,140,429,000	74.27%	$38.39	$23.95	1.6
3308	$48,371,000,000	$64,439,000,000	75.06%	$60.69	$36.05	1.68
2910	$15,219,000,000	$21,835,000,000	69.70%	$30.68	$30.75	1
3088	$2,551,501,000	$3,485,533,000	73.20%	$33.12	$23.80	1.39
2541	$7,445,500,000	$10,785,500,000	69.03%	$41.60	$29.13	1.43
9819	$2,648,136,000	$4,147,349,000	63.85%	$36.29	$21.08	1.72
2208	$26,118,000,000	$36,499,000,000	71.56%	$59.47	$38.82	1.53
2903	$22,266,609,000	$31,140,686,000	71.50%	$25.97	$17.52	1.48
7877	$3,560,763,000	$5,319,516,000	66.94%	$40.91	$33.09	1.24
6863	$7,250,600,000	$10,327,400,000	70.21%	$51.64	$38.54	1.34
7052	$34,962,000,000	$44,394,000,000	78.75%	$41.73	$30.76	1.36

Appendix O: Sample Firm Hypothesis 4 Dataset

Sample of 16 coded sample firms (H0: 4 data set for analysis)

Year	Avg. $((R_{it}) - (R_{ft}))$	$E(R_{Mt}) - R_{ft}$	$E(SMB_t)$	$E(HML_t)$
2010	15.04	17.39	13.52	-3.26
2011	0.41	0.47	-6.03	-6.58
2012	14.09	16.29	0.55	7.76

Data plugs for $E(R_{Mt}) - R_{ft}$, $E(SMB_t)$, and $E(HML_t)$ were retrieved from:

http://mba.tuck.dartmouth.edu/pages/faculty/ken.french/).

Avg. $((R_{it}) - (R_{ft}))$ was computed by subtracting the risk-free rate data plug from the 16

firm sample average (for each year) expected return computed from the capital asset

pricing model (CAPM).

Appendix P: Sample Firm Hypothesis 5 Dataset

CIK	2012_j-index	Adj_NTRFP4_2012	CMVCP5_2012	CMC6_2012
2224	-36.748	0.52	-7.9	$16,661,056,720
6160	-34.788	0.62	-9.98	$44,956,914,099
3068	-29.248	0.5	-15.51	$3,118,657,327
0464	-23.548	0.64	-21.22	$1,607,060,295
1728	-25.178	1.17	-19.57	$1,177,639,856
1138	-30.388	0.57	-14.37	$1,755,614,015
3308	-33.978	0.61	-10.78	$29,327,379,041
2910	-29.738	0.49	-15.09	$7,453,737,093
3088	-29.578	0.51	-15.18	$1,293,433,657
2541	-30.718	0.65	-14.04	$4,873,611,473
9819	-29.738	0.96	-15.01	$2,414,871,927
2208	-30.878	0.67	-13.88	$17,259,049,707
2903	-34.138	0.59	-10.62	$13,042,066,174
7877	-26.808	0.61	-17.95	$2,173,717,084
6863	-27.948	0.56	-16.81	$4,094,052,595
7052	-36.748	0.42	-8.05	$14,723,408,399

Appendix Q: Formulaic Key

Determination of the Central Index Key (CIK) sample company codes.

The 10-digit CIK from the U.S. Securities and Exchange Commission's (SEC) EDGAR online database was truncated from 10 digits to the final four (e.g. 0000056789 to 6789).

Determination of the security Market Price (MP1) for each sample company.

The annual report for each sample company contained the end-of-the-year market price for the associated, publicly traded company's closing price, typically on December 31st.

Determination of the Book Price per share (BV2) for each sample company.

The annual report for each sample company contained the values for the equation: - BV2 = [Total Assets – (Intangible Assets + Total Liabilities)]/Common Shares Outstanding.

Determination of the Return-on-Assets (ROA3) for each sample company.

The annual report for each sample company contained the values for the equation: ROA3 = Net Income/Total Assets.

Determination of Market-to-Book (MVBV) (NTRFP4) for each sample company.

The annual report for each sample company contained the values for the equation: NTRFP4 = MP1/BV2.

Determination of the Variant Price (CMVCP5) for each sample company.

The annual report for each sample company and the online Ken French database contained values for the CAPM-based equation for the excess security return above and beyond the individual sample firms' ROA3 (effectively, excess return = ROA3 $- E(R_i)$: CMVCP5 = ROA3 $- ((R_{(ft)}) + (\beta * E(R_{Mt}) - (R_{(ft)})))$.

Appendix Q: Formulaic Key (continued)

Determination of sample company Market Capitalization (CMC6).

CMC6 = MP1 * Common Shares Outstanding.

Determination of the Beta (β) for each sample company.

βi = Cov(*Ri, Rm*)/Var(*Rm*).

Determination of the Adjusted Book Value (Adj_BV2) for each sample company.

Adj_BV2 = [(Total Assets + Amount Derivative Needed) – (Intangible Assets + Total Liabilities)]/Common Shares Outstanding.

Determination of the Adjusted Market-to-Book (MVBV) (Adj_NTRFP4) for each sample company.

Adj_NTRFP4 = MP1/Adj_BV2.

Determination of the Amount Derivative Needed (Amt_Deriv_needed) for each sample company to bring sample firm from present debt-ratio to 50% debt-ratio.

Amt_Deriv_needed = (Total Liabilities * 2) – Total Assets.

Determination of the Fama-French Theoretical Equation Rectifier (j-index) for each sample company.

j-index = Calculated Sample Firm's Excess Return – Fama-French Equation's Rectified Result

Curriculum Vitae

EDUCATION

Walden University

Ph.D., Doctor of Philosophy in Management, August 2013

Major: Financial Economics

Dissertation: "Relative Pricing of Publicly Traded U.S. Electric Utility Company Securities."

The principal investigator's goal for this study was to demonstrate that there was a relationship between the independent variables of market value and book value to ROA and that the relationship would indicate, consistent with the undervaluation or overvaluation of publicly traded U.S. electric utility company securities, whether or not those securities would be appropriate for inclusion in an entity's investment portfolio (individual investors, financial intermediaries, and portfolio managers). The use of a study-based Excel computer model process and a multiple regression equation induced financial index to conduct a business intercession for the debt-ratio reduction of these firms has larger applications in the current macroeconomy concerning the reduction of a nation's debt-ratio versus the raising of a nation's debt ceiling.

Additional Research Project: "Corporate officer's symposium for international trade."

Implications for Positive, Constructive, Social Change: The contemporary purpose of this application construct was the prospective enlightenment of corporate "C-class" officers so that these officers were more aware of the constructive choices available for international trade. These officers would then be better informed to effectively conduct such trade in order to promote global "win-win" trading between nations.

Additional Research Project: "Compliancy symposium for bankers."

Implications for Positive, Constructive, Social Change: The contemporary purpose of this application construct was the prospective enforcement of regulatory compliancy with the theoretical, prospective requirements for central bank fiscal reporting transparency after central bank independence.

Additional Research Project: "An econometric construct for use in economic forecasting."

Implications for Positive, Constructive, Social Change: The contemporary purpose of this application construct was the development of a theoretical, overall structure of how an economic computer model could be used in an application to conduct economic forecasting. Although this may prove to be a platform for further research, it was postulated that further research was necessary in this field to promote the development of a useful tool for practical application.

The New York Institute of Technology   Old Westbury, NY

M.B.A., 2008, Major: Finance (Graduated with Distinction)

[Ellis College]

Southern Illinois University   Carbondale, IL

B.S., 1984, Major: Technical Careers (Health Care Services)

[Management Program]

Universal Accounting Center   Salt Lake City, UT

Full-Charge Bookkeeper Certification

[Board Certification - June 2006]

Universal Accounting Center   Salt Lake City, UT

Tax Preparer Certification

[Board Certification - July 2006]

INTERESTS

Research: International Finance, International Trade, Firm Valuation, Export Finance.

Teaching: Macroeconomics, Microeconomics, Global Finance, Derivatives,

Management, Trade.

COMMUNITY AND VOLUNTEER ACTIVITIES

Federal neutral arbitrator and judge for the Financial Industry Regulatory Authority

      (FINRA), the independent regulator for all securities firms doing business in the

      United States. FINRA Dispute Resolution Arbitrator ID: A58944.

Radio Talk Show Host – Host and moderator of a radio talk show entitled *Memphis*

      Money that airs every Saturday afternoon in Memphis, Tennessee on CBS affiliate

      990 AM KWAM Talk Radio. This is a weekly community development talk show

      that hosts interviews with local leaders and the moderator seeks answers to

      questions concerning the leaders' plans for local growth and economic

      development.

Adult Sunday School Teacher – The congregation where we attend church

Finance Committee Member - The congregation where we attend church

International Judge - SIFMA Foundation for Investor Education -

www.investwrite.org/judges

NON-FICTION BOOKS PUBLISHED

Jewczyn, N. (2010). *International trade: Traditional theory, current research, and*

   practical application. iUniverse: New York, NY.

Jewczyn, N. (2009). *Macroeconomic issues: Their relationship to fiscal policy*

   formulation, forecasting, prediction, and computer simulation modeling.

   iUniverse: New York, NY.

Jewczyn, N. (2009). *Behavioral psychology and educational counseling: An overview of*

   selected origins, current research and the application implications for the

   academic and career counseling of college students. iUniverse: New York, NY.

FICTION BOOKS PUBLISHED

Jewczyn, N. (2011). *Seven before the world.* AuthorHouse: New York, NY.

BOARD APPOINTMENTS TO PEER-REVIEWED JOURNALS

Jewczyn, N. (2011). Appointed to the editorial board of the *Asian Journal of Scientific*

   Research, eISSN: 2077-2076, as Technical Editor. Science Alert, New York,

   N.Y. Retrieved from http://scialert.net/eboardlivedna.php?issn=1992-

   1454&id=1.3143

Jewczyn, N. (2011). Appointed to the editorial board of the *Journal of Applied Sciences,*

   eISSN: 1812-5662, as Technical Editor. Science Alert, New York, N.Y.

229

Retrieved from http://scialert.net/eboardlivedna.php?issn=1812-5654&id=1.3143

Jewczyn, N. (2011). Appointed to the editorial board of the *Research Journal of Business Management,* eISSN: 2152-0437, as Technical Editor. Science Alert, New York, N.Y. Retrieved from http://scialert.net/eboardlivedna.php?issn=1819-1932&id=1.3143

Jewczyn, N. (2011). Appointed to the editorial board of the *The International Journal of Applied Economics and Finance*, eISSN: 2077-2149, as Technical Editor. Science Alert, New York, N.Y. Retrieved from http://scialert.net/eboardlivedna.php?issn=1991-0886&id=1.3143

Jewczyn, N. (2011). Appointed to the editorial board of the journal of *Trends in Applied Sciences Research,* eISSN: 2151-7908, as Technical Editor. Science Alert, New York, N.Y. Retrieved from http://scialert.net/eboardlivedna.php?issn=1819-3579&id=1.3143

PEER-REVIEWED JOURNAL PUBLICATIONS

Jewczyn, N. (2013). The finance of public pension funds, EVT portfolio theory, and application. *The Mustang Journal of Accounting and Finance, 3*(5), 56-64.

Jewczyn, N. (2013). Theory guidance in social science and finance application. *The International Journal of Social Science Research, 1*(1), 72-83.

Jewczyn, N. (2010). The use of derivatives: Earning only a limited premium and the elimination of upside risk. *The Journal of Business Management and*

Entrepreneurship, 1(11), 1-9.

Jewczyn, N. (2010). Some finance implications of the collapse of the Argentine currency board. *The Journal of Business Management and Entrepreneurship, 1*(10), 1-10.

Jewczyn, N. (2010). Finance considerations of the international Fisher effect: Manifestations in the short-run and the long-run. *The Journal of Business Management and Entrepreneurship, 1*(9), 1-9.

Jewczyn, N. (2010). A comparison of equity theory and expectancy theory and some implications for managers in a global work environment. *The Journal of Business Management and Entrepreneurship, 1*(8), 1-11.

Jewczyn, N. (2010). Integrative business policy with a SWOT analysis of Southwest Airlines: What are they doing right in today's economy? *The Journal of Business Leadership Today, 1*(8), 1-14.

Jewczyn, N. (2010). Contemporary global commerce and global warming: Insights into Al Gore's documentary *An Inconvenient Truth. The Journal of Business Leadership Today, 1*(7), 1-10.

Jewczyn, N. (2010). Principles of character in leadership: Former General Electric CEO Jack Welch as an inspiration for future corporate leadership. *The Journal of Online Higher Education 1*(7), 1-12.

Jewczyn, N. (2010). Assessing mechanistic and organic organizational structures: Measuring organizational uncertainty and determining an organization's proper structure. *The Journal of Business Management and Entrepreneurship, 1*(6), 1-12.

Jewczyn, N. (2010). Job satisfaction, morale, and cultural diversity: Factors

    influencing worker perspectives, expectations, and management strategies. *The*

    Journal of Virtual Leadership, 1(6), 1-11.

    <u>Public archive of publications is available at:</u>   http://www.researchgate.net

PEER-REVIEWED CONFERENCE PRESENTATIONS

Jewczyn, N. (2011). *An organizational conflict and negotiation literature review and*

    annotated bibliography. 2011 Winter International Conference of the

    International Organization of Social Sciences and Behavioral Research

    (IOSSBR), Planet Hollywood, Las Vegas, NV, U.S.A.

Jewczyn, N. (2011). *Liquidity risk exposure and the types of risks associated with*

    financial intermediaries. 2011 Winter International Conference of the

    International Organization of Social Sciences and Behavioral Research

    (IOSSBR), Planet Hollywood, Las Vegas, NV, U.S.A.

Jewczyn, N. (2011). *Macroeconomic money movement: The risks common to financial*

    intermediaries and the associated regulatory implications. 2011 Winter

    International Conference of the International Organization of Social Sciences and

    Behavioral Research (IOSSBR), Planet Hollywood, Las Vegas, NV, U.S.A.

Jewczyn, N. (2011). *The grocery wars: Wal-Mart, Whole Foods Market, and Kroger*

    compete for marketshare. 2011 Winter International Conference of the

    International Organization of Social Sciences and Behavioral Research

    (IOSSBR), Planet Hollywood, Las Vegas, NV, U.S.A.

Jewczyn, N. (2011). *International risk exposures of financial intermediary balance sheet structures and the impact of domestic securities regulation.* 2011 Program for the Academy of Business Research (ABR), Trump Plaza, Atlantic City, NJ.

Jewczyn, N. (2011). *The global integration of capital markets and a strategy to capture lower cost capital.* 2011 Program for the Academy of Business Research (ABR), Trump Plaza, Atlantic City, NJ.

Jewczyn, N. (2010). *International trade theory comparisons and trade as an implement of national, foreign policy.* 2010 International Colloquium on Business & Management (ICBM), Bangkok, Thailand. Featured presenter.

Jewczyn, N. (2009). *Implications of a partial synthesis secondary to the Isard gravity model of trade contrasted with Paul Krugman's new trade theory.* 2009 International Conference on Applied Business and Economics (ICABE), Kavala, Greece.

Jewczyn, N. (2009). *Central banks as economic institutions in the aggregate economy.* 2009 International Business & Economics Research Conference, Las Vegas, Nevada.

Jewczyn, N. (2009). *A survey of the international economics implications of the ascension of monetary policy independence and the reporting transparency of national, central banks.* 2009 International Conference on Innovative Strategies for Value Creation and Management, (RVIM), Bangalore, India

REVIEW COMMITTEE MEMBER FOR PEER-REVIEWED

    JOURNALS

(2010). Journal of Public Service eLearning (JOPSE)

(2010). The Journal of Business Leadership Today (JOBLT)

(2010). The Journal of Business Management and Entrepreneurship (JOBME)

PEER-REVIEWED, PUBLISHED, CONFERENCE PROCEEDINGS

2011 Program for the Academy of Business Research (ABR), Proceedings of the International Academy of Business Research Fall Conference (ABR), Atlantic City, NJ. *International risk exposures of financial intermediary balance sheet structures and the impact of domestic securities regulation.*

2011 Program for the Academy of Business Research (ABR), Proceedings of the International Academy of Business Research Fall Conference (ABR), Atlantic City, NJ. *The global integration of capital markets and a strategy to capture lower cost capital.*

2010 International Colloquium on Business & Management (ICBM), Proceedings of the 3rd International Colloquium on Business & Management (ICBM), Bangkok, Thailand. *International trade theory comparisons and trade as an implement of national, foreign policy.* ISBN: 978-0-9864591-7-7, Nicholas.Jewczyn.ICBM.2010.58.RP.pdf v.2, 2010.

2009 International Business & Economics Research Conference (IBER) - 9th Annual Conference Proceedings Publication. *Central banks as economic institutions in the aggregate economy.*

http://cluteinstitute.com/Programs/Las_Vegas_2009/index.htm.

2009 International Conference on Applied Business and Economics (ICABE) - Annual
Conference Proceedings Publication, Kavala, Greece. *Implications of a partial
synthesis secondary to the Isard gravity model of trade contrasted with Paul
Krugman's new trade theory.* ISSN: 1108-2976, P. 89, (2009).
http://www.icabe.gr/downloads/ICABE_2009_PROC.pdf.

2009 International Conference on Innovative Strategies for Value Creation and
Management, (RVIM), RVIM Journal of Management Research, Bangalore,
India. *A survey of the international economics implications of the ascension of
monetary policy independence and the reporting transparency of national, central
banks.* ISSN: 0974-6722, SI 43, (2009).

CONFERENCES

2011 Program for the Academy of Business Research (ABR), Research Presentation
Sessions of the International Academy of Business Research Fall Conference,
Atlantic City, NJ. Session Chair on Thursday morning September 15th of the
Chelsea A presentation room in the field of education, representing Northcentral
University. Presentation room sponsored by Cabell's.

2011 Program for the Academy of Business Research (ABR), Research Presentation
Sessions of the International Academy of Business Research Fall Conference,
Atlantic City, NJ. Session Chair on Thursday afternoon September 15th of the

Westminster C presentation room in the field of accounting,

representing Northcentral University. Presentation room sponsored by the

A.A.C.S.B.

2010 Innovative Professional Practices, Synergy, and eCollaboration, an International

Conference virtually conducted by the eLearning Institute.

2010 DeVry University/Keller School of Management update faculty training to move

online, hybrid, and onsite teaching modes from the iOptimize to the eCollege

teaching platform.

2010 International Colloquium on Business & Management (ICBM), Bangkok, Thailand.

2009 International Conference on Applied Business and Economics (ICABE), Kavala,

Greece.

2009 International Business & Economics Research Conference, Las Vegas, Nevada.

2009 College Teaching and Learning Conference, Las Vegas, Nevada.

2009 International Conference on Innovative Strategies for Value Creation and

Management, (RVIM), Bangalore, India.

RESIDENCIES AND SYMPOSIA

2009 - **Milestone 4 Doctoral Residency** - Jacksonville, FL (September 30 - October 4)

Workshop Themes - Focus upon research skills for the conduct of studies,

dissertation skills, academic and professional publishing, and *Social Change*

Through Research.

2009 - **Milestone 3 Doctoral Residency** - Minneapolis, MN (July 19 - 25)

Workshop Themes - Focus upon research skills for the writing of a doctoral prospectus and proposal, dissertation skills, and *Scholarship at the Doctoral Level*.

2009 - **Milestone 2 Doctoral Residency** - Dallas, TX (January 18 - 24)

Workshop Themes - Focus upon research skills for the conduct of studies, doctoral level applied statistics for use in the dissertation and studies, and *Skills for Doctoral Research*.

2008 - **Milestone 1 Doctoral Residency** - St. Charles, IL (October 15 - 19)

Workshop Themes - Focus upon research skills for the de-mystification of the Knowledge Area Module Process, and *Socialization into the Walden Community*.

TEACHING EXPERIENCE

The American College

Online Virtual Campus

2013 Fall Term

Instructor, FA 200 - Techniques for Prospecting: Prospect or Perish (LUTCF designation sequence of courses)

Eastern University

Online Virtual Campus

2013 Fall Term

Instructor, Business Mathematical Finance 360 (Business Baccalaureate in Professional Studies Class), Cohort Group #48OCJA-13, Class BUS360 OCJA13S43, 3 semester hours

2013 Summer Term

Instructor, Business Mathematical Finance 360 (Business Baccalaureate in Professional

Studies Class), Cohort Group #43APLJ-13, Class BUS360APLJ13S43, 3

semester hours

Bethel University

Memphis, Tennessee Campus

2011 Fall Term

Instructor, Strategic Planning (Business Baccalaureate Degree Capstone Class), MOD

440, Cohort Group #56, Class 1456-11, 3 semester hours

The National College of Business and Technology

Memphis, Tennessee Campus

2010 Fall Term I (August 30, 2010 - November 13, 2010)

Instructor, BUS-121-2, Principles of Economics, 4 quarter hours

Instructor, ACC-320-4, Intermediate Accounting II, 4 quarter hours

Instructor, MAT-210-5, Business Mathematics (Finance), 4 quarter hours

Instructor, ACC-203-B, Cost Accounting I, 4 quarter hours

Instructor, MAT-210-E, Business Mathematics (Finance), 4 quarter hours

The National College of Business and Technology

Bartlett, Tennessee Campus

2008 Winter Term II (December 29, 2008 - March 7, 2009)

Instructor, BUS-121-B, Principles of Economics, 4 quarter hours

Instructor, BUS-121-5, Principles of Economics, 4 quarter hours

Instructor, ACC-101-C, College Accounting I, 4 quarter hours

The National College of Business and Technology

Bartlett, Tennessee Campus

2008 Winter Term I (December 1, 2008 - February 22, 2009)

Instructor, ACC-101-1, College Accounting I, 4 quarter hours

Instructor, ACC-101-A2, College Accounting I, 4 quarter hours

Instructor, ACC-102-2, College Accounting II, 4 quarter hours

Instructor, ACC-216-4, Principles of Taxation, 4 quarter hours

DeVry University

Memphis, Tennessee Campus

2008 Fall Term (8) 2008 (October 27, 2008 - December 21, 2008)

Instructor, ECON-312, Principles of Economics, 3 semester hours

The National College of Business and Technology

Memphis, Tennessee Campus

2008 Fall Term II (October 6, 2008 - December 13, 2008)

Instructor, BUS-101-1, Introduction to Business, 4 quarter hours

The National College of Business and Technology

Memphis, Tennessee Campus

2008 Fall Term I (September 2, 2008 - November 22, 2008)

Instructor, ACC-320-1, Intermediate Accounting II, 4 quarter hours

The National College of Business and Technology

Bartlett, Tennessee Campus

2008 Fall Term I (September 2, 2008 - November 22, 2008)

Instructor, ACC-101-1, College Accounting I, 4 quarter hours

Instructor, ACC-110-2, Payroll Accounting, 4 quarter hours

Instructor, CRT-150-B, Introduction to Critical Thinking, 4 quarter hours

Instructor, MAT-210-C, Business Mathematics (Finance), 4 quarter hours

MEMBERSHIPS AND PROFESSIONAL AFFILIATIONS

American Economic Association – Nashville, Tennessee -

http://www.vanderbilt.edu/AEA

American Finance Association - Berkeley, California - http://www.afajof.org

Omicron Delta Epsilon (Beta Delta Chapter) – Hattiesburg, Mississippi -

http://www.omicrondeltaepsilon.org

Sigma Iota Epsilon International (Zeta Rho Chapter) - Ft. Collins, Colorado -

http://www.sienational.com

AWARDS

2012 (March) Inducted into Delta Mu Delta Honor Society for Excellence in Business

Studies as a doctoral student – Delta Mu Delta Honors Stole and suspension

medal to be worn as part of graduation regalia when receiving the Ph.D. as an

honors graduate of Northcentral University (along with the society charter and an honors fraternity key).

2011 Inducted into Golden Key Scholastic Honor Society for Excellence in Business and Finance Studies as a doctoral student, in September 2011 - awarded the Golden Key Honors Stole to be worn as part of graduation regalia when receiving the Ph.D. as an honors graduate of Northcentral University (along with the society charter and an honors fraternity key).

2009 Inducted into Sigma Iota Epsilon Professional and Honorary Management Fraternity for Excellence in Management Studies as a doctoral student and for academic publishing, in July 2009 - awarded the SIE Honors Stole to be worn as part of graduation regalia when receiving the Ph.D. as an honors graduate of Walden University (along with the fraternity charter and a professional fraternity key).

2009 Inducted into Phi Delta Kappa Professional Fraternity for College Teaching Excellence in January 2009 - awarded a certificate and professional fraternity key.

2007 Inducted into Omicron Delta Epsilon Scholastic Fraternity for Excellence as a graduate student in the Field of Economics, in August 2007 - awarded the ODE Honors Stole that was worn as part of graduation regalia when the M.B.A. was received as an honors graduate of the New York Institute of Technology (along with the scroll plaque, a professional fraternity key, and a suspension medal).

PATENTS

2007 **United States Patent and Trademark Office** - Provisional Patent Number

60/972,675

Granted for The Myloi Process on September 25, 2007.

CONSULTING

2009 Memphis, Tennessee. Private Consulting Firm (*confidential*). Invited by a consulting firm to deal with a difficult client. Financials and *pro forma* were re-aligned to return the client to a profit-making stance - improved client manufacturing efficiency by 28% and re-tooled the client's ten-year *pro forma* concerning mergers/acquisitions and the introduction of potentially unprofitable product lines. Consulting deliverables were provided to the client on a fee-for-service basis (for a confidential amount). Versions of the Executive Summary, common-sized, multi-year financials, and the tabular data (organized by product SIC codes) were delivered to the private corporation's board.

2008 Washington, D.C. Invited by the American Economic Association, as a professional Economist, to comment on the Public Principles and Guidelines Revisions of the *Water Resources Development Act of 2007*, known as *Public Law 110-114.* Report published October 2008:

http://www.usace.army.mil/cw/hot_topics/ht_2008/pandg_rev.htm.

Consulting services Executive Summary provided to the United States Army Corps of Engineers and the United States Government as a courtesy free of charge.

2007 Private Technical College. Was called in to consult with the college president concerning the apparent lack of student progress toward graduation

and the continued use of antiquated, laboratory equipment. Wrote an Executive

Summary that, when applied, improved the use of the technical labs by over 40%

and the modular lesson plan format, from the summary, shortened the time to

student graduation by over 20%. Consulting provided by contract for: an initial

retainer plus $250 per hour plus expenses. Executive Summary was deemed by

the Board to be proprietary and is unavailable for public dissemination.

RESEARCH QUALIFICATIONS

2013 The National Institutes of Health (NIH) Office of Extramural Research certified

research competence on February 14, 2013 - Certificate Number 1119993 (based

upon satisfactory completion of the course of study and examinations prescribed

by the United States government course for researchers entitled, "Protecting

Human Research Participants").

2011 Collaborative Institutional Training Initiative (CITI) - Human Research Curriculum

Completion certified research competence on May 6, 2011 - Report Reference

Number 5982040. Dissertation FMD Training – Required Modules - Belmont

Report and CITI Course Introduction (100%), History and Ethical Principles –

SBR (100%), Defining Research with Human Subjects – SBR (100%), The

Regulations and The Social and Behavioral Sciences – SBR (100%), Assessing

Risk in Social and Behavioral Sciences – SBR (100%), Informed Consent – SBR

(100%), Privacy and Confidentiality – SBR (100%), Research with Children –

SBR (100%), Research in Public Elementary and Secondary Schools –

SBR (100%), International Research – SBR (100%), International Studies

(100%), Internet Research – SBR (100%), Workers as Research Subjects-A

Vulnerable Population (100%), Conflicts of Interest in Research Involving

Human Subjects (100%), The IRB Member Module - "What Every New IRB

Member Needs to Know" (100%), and the Northcentral University module.

2009 The National Institutes of Health (NIH) Office of Extramural Research certified

research competence on April 8, 2009 - Certificate Number 214161 (based upon

satisfactory completion of the course of study and examinations prescribed by the

United States government course for researchers entitled, "Protecting Human

Research Participants").

COURSE AND CURRICULUM DEVELOPMENT

The National College of Business and Technology

COURSE DEVELOPMENT

All courses taught at this institution required the development of an individualized

prospectus. A prospectus for each course taught at these campuses is available

upon request.

GRADING PLATFORM

Developed and wrote the computer software that was accepted by both campuses

in the Memphis, Tennessee area (at the request of the Program Director over the

Bartlett Campus). The computer grading platform became required for use by all instructors (for grade submission at the conclusion of each term) at both campuses and this instructor taught the mandatory professional development courses to instruct the faculty at both campuses in the use of that grading software package.

APPLICATIONS DEVELOPMENT

Developed and wrote the computer software that was used as an Accounting Class remedial intervention to: A) provide remedial support as a self-paced, Accounting Laboratory workshop to supplement the class texts; B) provide laboratory drills to support more advanced Accounting skills in journalizing and posting to prepare the students for my class term project (the development of a corporation's set of financial statements); C) provide an assessment instrument for the Director of Student Services when an Accounting Class tutor was necessary (to demonstrate weak areas where the student needed an additional focus from the assigned tutor).

COLLEGE LEVEL TEACHING QUALIFICATIONS

The National College Administration, upon evaluation of all official college transcripts and, upon the advice and consent of the A.C.I.C.S. Accreditation Board, has given certification as an instructor to teach the Accounting, Business, Finance, and Economics classes, at 25 college campuses, at the Associate's, Bachelor's, and Master of Business Administration levels. Course certification lists available upon request.

DeVry University

Developed the syllabus, course content, grading platform and testing media for the Economics 312 course taught at the Memphis, Tennessee campus. Further, developed the hybrid online platform of all computerized content, the discussion platform, and automated testing media utilized in the course.

Walden University

This doctoral student was allowed to create, develop, and pursue his own Self-Designed, Ph.D. Business Management Program with a specialization in International Economics.

COLLEGE FACULTY AND FINANCE CONTINUING EDUCATION

Financial Services Industry Training and Continuing Education

January and February 2011

State of Tennessee specific professional or continuing education courses completed.

Agent Practices (06_05PMIC)

Agent's Guide to Anti-Money Laundering (01_08PMIC)

Annuities (01_05PMIC)

Cancer Protection with Critical Illness Options (07PMIC_01)

Life Insurance (09_05PMIC)

Medicare Supplement (05_05PMIC)

Prospecting (08_05PMIC)

Science of Selling (03_05PMIC)

Vista Care Choices LTC1 (02_05PMIC)

246

An Overview of Business Insurance (eLIBI)

An Overview of Group Insurance (eLIGI)

An Overview of Health Insurance (eLIHI)

An Overview of Term & Permanent Insurance (eLITPI)

An Overview of the Life Insurance Sales Cycle (eLIOLS)

Annuities (eLIANN)

Basic Background for Needs Selling (eLIBN)

Buy/Sell Agreements (eLIBSA)

California Long-Term Care (eLICLTC)

Disability Income Insurance (eLIDI)

Introduction to HIPAA (eLIHIPAA)

Long Term Care: An In-Depth View (146)

Medicaid (eLIMDD)

Medicaid - Second Edition (162_2)

Medicare - Second Edition (161_2)

Medigap - Second Edition (160_2)

Sales Training (eLIST)

Senior Protection in Annuity Transactions Model Regulation (91)

Suitability of Annuity Transactions - Texas (263)

Texas 4-Hour Annuity Certification Course (263_Cert)

Universal Life Insurance (eLIUL)

November 2010

LTC Partnership Course Training for Financial Professionals.

8 credit hours awarded for the completion of LTC Connection's (an authorized provider

for The Department of Commerce and Insurance) course, which meets DRA and

NAIC requirements for certification of financial professionals in the Long-Term

Care Industry. Continuing Education Certification.

October 2010

National Anti-Money Laundering Training for Financial Professionals.

Training mandated by the National Association of Insurance Commissioners

(NAIC), to comply with federal regulations concerning general rules of antitrust

compliance. Training administered by the Life Insurance and Market Research

Association (LIMRA), now commonly known as LIMRA International, Inc.

The National College of Business and Technology

September 2010

.7 CEUs awarded for the completion of Cengage Learnings's (an authorized

provider of the International Association of Continuing Education and Training

(IACET) for faculty) *Module 7 - Teaching Students How to Learn.*

September 2010

.7 CEUs awarded for the completion of Cengage Learnings's (an authorized

provider of the International Association of Continuing Education and Training

(IACET) for faculty) *Module 10 - Customer Service in the Classroom.*

DeVry University

Spring 2010

Faculty update training for the in-transition preparation for the new hybrid teaching platform integration - a model that stresses a combination of online and onsite teaching methods, technologies, and faculty administration.

PROFESSIONAL EXPERIENCE

January 2012 – Present *Private Wealth Manager* **– Securities Brokerage - Memphis, TN**

Stock broker and portfolio manager who works with clients on a daily basis to perform: financial planning, portfolio management, and legacy functions.

Licenses held:

General Securities Representative – Series 7- FINRA

Futures Managed Funds – Series 31- FINRA

Uniform Combined State Law – Series 66 - FINRA

Variable Life and Health Insurance License – Tennessee, Mississippi, and Arkansas

Property and Casualty Insurance License - Tennessee, Mississippi, and Arkansas

November 2010 – December 2011 *Agency Development Manager* **- Germantown, TN**

General Agent for the marketing of group and individual life and health insurance coverage for individuals, families, and companies. Implementation of buy-sell agreement coverage involving private insurance or stock transfers secondary to business succession for businesses that have 5 - 10 partners. Marketing

of true group coverage for small businesses of up to 100 employees in the general

market. Sales of major medical policies and ordinary debit coverage for families

and individuals. Installment of retirement plans that involve the sales and

marketing of fixed or fixed index annuities. Recruiting, appointment, and training

of agents in Tennessee and Mississippi to market our agency's products.

August 2008 - November 2010   National College of Business and Technology

Faculty **- Memphis, Tennessee**

Adjunct faculty at a college that grants Associate's, Bachelor's, and Master's

Degrees (M.B.A.). Primary responsibilities include: course content coordination;

course content updates and accreditation; course content review, supplementation

and revision; student advising and various other traditional activities including

school promotional activities, retention, and administration. Part of my

responsibility is to make certain that students complete all core requirements to

make ready for graduation. Wrote, implemented, and trained faculty in the use of

the software grading platform that is now in required use at all 25 campuses.

March 2001- August 2006   Kastane Agency – *Principal* – Germantown, TN

Started as an agent marketing Life and Health insurance locally in the Memphis,

Tennessee area. With transferability of results gained from previous business

positions, was able to grow the agency from a single agent to over 100 agents (at

close of business) who represented three dozen companies marketing Life and

Health insurance to thousands of clients and businesses in a three state area. During most of the agency's existence, there were typically between one and two dozen agents active at any one time in my agency. Before closing the business, in order to return to college and obtain a Master's Degree, was promoted to Senior, Master General Agent who supervised Regional Managers, District Managers and Sales Managers. Responsible for agency production, the writing, and the enforcement of contracts directly to insurance company Presidents.